# Stalk Yourself:
## A Guide to Information Collection, Privacy and Defending Yourself

Andrew Meyers

"If you know the enemy and know yourself you need not fear the results of a hundred battles."

- Sun Tzu
The Art of War

# CONTENTS

# ACKNOWLEDGMENTS

Thanks to my beautiful wife Rachel for helping make this book possible.

# INTRODUCTION

In today's age of computer systems, our entire lives are increasingly stored into databases of some type. Every time we purchase an item at the grocery store with our discount card, our shopping habits are cataloged. This cataloging allows the grocery store to target you with specific advertisements.

Because technology is part of our everyday lives, people's concern with privacy has continually been at the top of news outlets, especially when it involves technology. The Health Insurance Portability and Accountability Act (HIPAA) is one such outcome to the privacy issue within the health care world. HIPAA restricts the sharing of information and what type of information can be shared only after the authorization of the patient. Recently, the popular social media website Facebook has been a large center of concern. The sharing of users' information with other websites and companies has many people worried about their individual privacy.

With all the concern people have placed on privacy issues, the invention the Internet, database technology, and the fusing of the two make it easier than ever to find information about an individual.

Even if someone does not use computers or smart phones, individuals still make it easy for others to gather information about them. People volunteer information in many different ways. Often they are oblivious to the information they freely share with the world. The trained mind however, can pick up on this.

This book describes offensive methods to gather information about a person. By showing you how easy it can be to gather information on a person and how someone would exploit it, your awareness will increase about what you share with the world and the possible consequences. I will share tricks, tools, and sometimes even point out the obvious. It can all be used to piece together the larger picture of an individual's life.

This book is meant as a guide and awareness tool to help you defend yourself against information gathering techniques. Any use of these offensive techniques in an unethical manner is not recommended and use of any of these methods is at your own risk. This book, its author, and its publisher do not claim any responsibility for your individual decisions.

# 1

# INTERNET

The Internet was originally created to share information between U.S. defense computer systems. It was created to be resilient against attack or malfunction. If one system went down, the other systems were still able to operate and communicate. This concept has grown into something the original developers could never have imagined. The amount of information shared on the Internet continues to surprise us every day. The invention of social networking and social media has continued to push the limit. Although it may be obvious that information contained on the Internet is plentiful, many individuals may be stumped on how to actually go about finding information on an individual.

## Web Mining

Web mining refers to scouring different websites to collect information about a specific subject. Often these websites are created for information sharing and not nefarious purposes, however they can be used to collect information about an individual that may end up being used as such.

## Amazon.com Wish List

Amazon.com has created a feature to assist you in buying gifts for friends and loved ones. If a user has an account with Amazon.com, they can log into there profile and add products to their wish list. Friends and family type in the user's email address (the same being used for the Amazon.com's profile) and can view the user's wish list such as the one below.

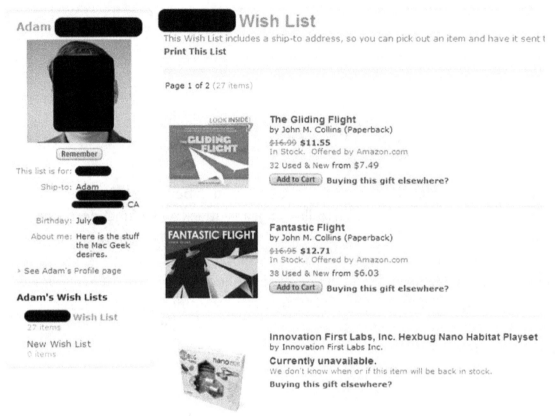

Figure 1-1

Information Collected:

1. Photo of target
2. Full name
3. Town of residence
4. Birthday without year
5. Target likes Apple computer (About Me section)
6. Target's reading interest and hobbies

Now that we can view the individual's wish list, we can look at the items and determine some of the their interests. In this case, we know the individual is interested in books on flight. Not shown in the picture is a list of Nintento Wii games and accessories, a Battlestar Galactica DVD and action figures. As you can see in the results above, not only did we score a list of this person's areas of interest, we also know what they look like. (I got this individual's email through a Google search. The individual was advertising their wish list so other would buy those gifts for him.)

## Carfax

Carfax is a website where potential car buyers can go to check on the history of a vehicle. This site is useful in determining if the car has ever been in a crash, flood or fire. The buyer can use this information to make a determination whether or not to proceed with purchasing the vehicle.

This site may not be the first choice for mining data about an individual, however depending on the collector's motivation (perhaps a targeted car scam) it could prove valuable. To obtain the report you simply need the vehicle identification number (VIN) from the vehicle. This can be obtained in many ways with the easiest being to walk up to the vehicle and writing it down. (The VIN is usually near the bottom corner of the windshield on the driver's side.)

| **CARFAX** Ownership History The number of owners is estimated | Owner 1 | Owner 2 |
|---|---|---|
| Year purchased | 2003 | 2006 |
| Type of owner | Personal | Personal |
| Estimated length of ownership | 3 yrs. 5 mo. | 3 yrs. 10 mo. |
| Owned in the following states/provinces | Massachusetts | Massachusetts |
| Estimated miles driven per year | 13,623/yr | 20,616/yr |
| Last reported odometer reading | 47,654 | 119,993 |

Figure 1-2

Figure 1-3

Information Collected:

1. Possible time of vehicle purchase
2. Length of vehicle ownership
3. Place of vehicle purchase
4. Possible time of vehicle accident
5. Odometer reading and estimated miles driven per year

The above photos are taken from a sample report on Carfax.com. As you can see this car has had two owners and has been through at least one recorded accident. If this car still belongs to the individual who was in the crash, this individual could fall victim to scams such as offering health coverage or collision protection.

## Employer Websites

Employer websites sometimes offer a searchable directory of employees. It will display information such as title, phone number and email address. Sometimes, especially in the case of executives, there will be a short biographic paragraph about the individual. These can prove informative as they sometimes tend to discuss the executives birth town, education, past employers or work experience and, in some cases, hobbies and family members. As the information gleaned from an executive's biography is obvious, let's take a look at one with less information.

**College of Humanities and Social Sciences Office**
Office: MP 20⬤
Office Phone Number: ⬛⬛⬛
Voice Mail: Voice Mail
Fax: ⬛⬛⬛
E-mail: b⬛⬛⬛edu

⬛⬛**, Beth**
Administrative Assistant

Figure 1-4

Information Collected:

1. Full name
2. Job title
3. Employer name
4. Office location
5. Office phone number
6. Office email address
7. Possible photograph of target

In the information we have collected above we have this individual's office number (possible physical security issue) and job title. From the office number we know where the target spends most of their time when not at home. From the job title we can infer several things. First, this person most likely does not have a college education. We can infer this because most people who have graduated college do not take positions as administrative assistants. Secondly, we can probably guess the person's salary does not exceed $50,000. For salary guessing other factors can be used such as job longevity and in this case whether or not this is a private or state university.

## Social Security Numbers

Social security numbers are commonly and naively used for identification purposes. People use social security numbers instead of names because they believe it masks who the individual is. Social security numbers are distributed by using a formula. The process for issuing social security numbers has changed over the years so the following information should be used only as a guideline to help determine someone's social security number.

The first three digits are known as the Area Number and are distributed based upon where the social security number was assigned. Most of the time this tends to be where the individual was born. The following is a chart from usatrace.com and shows which numbers are assigned to which geographical region.

| 001-003 | NEW HAMPSHIRE | 486-500 | MISSOURI |
|---------|---------------|---------|----------|
| 004-007 | MAINE | 501-502 | NORTH DAKOTA |
| 008-009 | VERMONT | 503-504 | SOUTH DAKOTA |
| 010-034 | MASSACHUSETTS | 505-508 | NEBRASKA |
| 035-039 | RHODE ISLAND | 509-515 | KANSAS |
| 040-049 | CONNECTICUT | 516-517 | MONTANA |
| 050-134 | NEW YORK | 518-519 | IDAHO |
| 135-158 | NEW JERSEY | 520 | WYOMING |
| 159-211 | PENNSYLVANIA | 521-524 | COLORADO |
| 212-220 | MARYLAND | 525 | NEW MEXICO |
| 221-222 | DELAWARE | 526-527 | ARIZONA |
| 223-231 | VIRGINIA | 528-529 | UTAH |
| 232-236 | WEST VIRGINIA | 530 | NEVADA |
| 232,237-246 | NORTH CAROLINA | 531-539 | WASHINGTON |
| 247-251 | SOUTH CAROLINA | 540-544 | OREGON |
| 252-260 | GEORGIA | 545-573 | CALIFORNIA |

| 261-267 | FLORIDA | 574 | ALASKA |
|---------|---------|-----|--------|
| 268-302 | OHIO | 575-576 | HAWAII |
| 303-317 | INDIANA | 577-579 | WASHINGTON D.C. |
| 318-361 | ILLINOIS | 580 | VIRGIN ISLANDS |
| 362-386 | MICHIGAN | 580-584 | PUERTO RICO |
| 387-399 | WISCONSIN | 585 | NEW MEXICO |
| 400-407 | KENTUCKY | 586 | AMERICAN SAMOA, GUAM |
| 408-415 | TENNESSEE | 587-588 | MISSISSIPPI |
| 416-424 | ALABAMA | 589-595 | FLORIDA |
| 425-428 | MISSISSIPPI | 596-599 | PUERTO RICO |
| 429-432 | ARKANSAS | 600-601 | ARIZONA |
| 433-439 | LOUISIANA | 602-626 | CALIFORNIA |
| 440-448 | OKLAHOMA | 627-645 | TEXAS |
| 449-467 | TEXAS | 646-647 | UTAH |
| 468-477 | MINNESOTA | 648-649 | NEW MEXICO |
| 478-485 | IOWA | 700-728 | ISSUED TO RAILROAD BOARD PRIOR TO 1963 (NO LONGER USED) |

Table 1-1

The middle two numbers are known as Group numbers. Since 1965 they are issued in chronological order within the Area code.

The last four numbers are known as the Serial number. This number is issued consecutively. This is the numbers that identifies the individual. Many times these are the numbers used because they are the most specific to an individual. However this exposes the person's social security because as you can see above there is a method to distribution. Credit card numbers are issued in a similar manner, however that subject is beyond the scope of this book.

# Resumes and Professional Life

The average person spends about a quarter of their lives working. That means when viewing a person's resume we are able to recreate approximately a quarter of how they spend their daily life. Many individuals, when creating a resume, put as much information about themselves and their previous employers as possible. Although detailed information is essential to finding a job, it can also be used to put together pieces of an individual's life.

Figure 1-5

Information Collected:

1. Full name
2. Home address

3. Home phone number
4. Email address
5. Current (and past) employment
6. Skills
7. Level and place of education
8. Place and time of residence
9. BONUS: Company computer systems used

The image of the resume above was found by using a simple Google search. As you can see we have plenty of information about this individual. We know where the person went to school, has a desire to learn more about computers, and even a home phone number and address. In addition to these nuggets of information about the individual, we know now that the company the individual works for uses an AS400 system for payroll and employee files. This information is of great use to a computer criminal.

## LinkedIn

Resumes are not the only way a person's professional life can expose information about their personal life. The website Linkedin.com helps an individual market themselves and network among other individuals in the same industry. This site is great for data miners because, not only do individuals post a photo and information from their resume, they also link themselves to groups and companies and provide a short biography about themselves.

**Adam ⬛⬛⬛'s Summary**

Adam works with business owners, executives and their other professional advisors to design benefit programs that help them meet a variety of needs including employee retention and recruitment, tax and retirement planning and business succession. He assists companies in assessing benefit programs as part of mergers, acquisitions and other similar business transactions. In addition, he works with clients to address plan errors under the IRS and Department of Labor correction programs.

Adam serves on ⬛⬛⬛ national board of directors as well as the ⬛⬛⬛

**Figure 1-6**

Information Collected:

1. Target photograph
2. Full name
3. City of residence
4. Job title
5. Current and past employment
6. Level and places of education
7. Target's job responsibilities and possibly more in Summary

If you create a free account, you can see much more information about this individual. You can view whom the individual recommends (showing a relationship between the two people), what other profiles were viewed similar to this individual, and social networking websites. (Hopefully you didn't post anything too telling on your Facebook page.)

Depending on how dedicated you are to exploit this individual, you can pay for a membership and receive even more information. One of these features includes showing other people whom both you and the individual know; something military analysts call an association matrix.

## Classmates.com

With the constant pop-up and banner advertisements of the early 2000's, everyone is probably already familiar with classmates.com. Since most people have already seen this web site and knows how it works it will be described in brief.

Classmates.com describes their website as having the ability to "Find friends and alumni, preview yearbooks, browse nostalgic photos, and reconnect with the past." This is exactly what an information collector would be looking for. A simple search for your target could yield a wealth of past information, depending on how much information they were willing to enter into the website's database. A sizable chunk of a person's life could be revealed through this website.

# Public Records

The idea of skimming information from public records should be a no brainer. However, the combination of the information present on public records and the ubiquity of the Internet have the potential to create a bad day for someone. Some counties in the United States have taken it upon themselves to upload public records, some dating as far back as 1978, to the public Internet.

The following images show how easy it can be to gain access to almost any type of public record in this particular county, even giving the user directions.

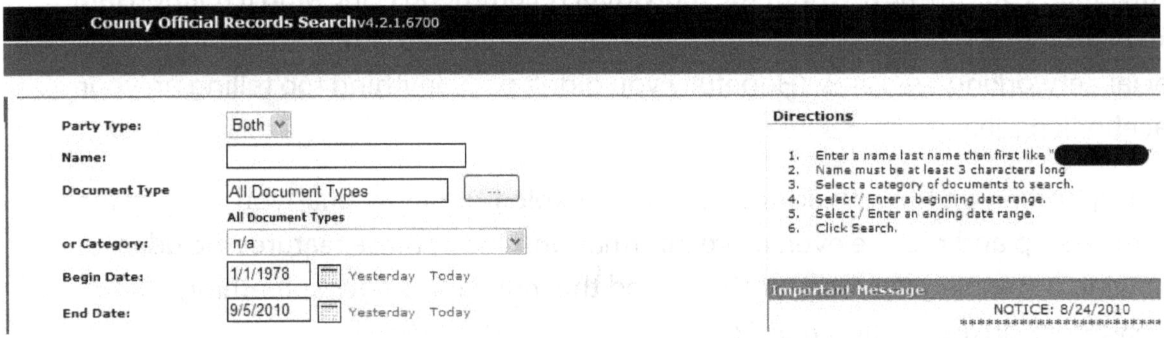

Figure 1-7

Figure 1-8

After a simple search we can see these individuals have legally established a domestic partnership.

**DECLARATION OF DOMESTIC PARTNERSHIP**

We swear or affirm under penalty of perjury that:

1. We are both 18 or older and competent to contract;

2. Neither of us is married nor a partner to another domestic partnership relationship;

3. Neither of us is related to the other by blood;

4. We are domiciled in ▉▉▉ County, or are, otherwise, subject to the provisions of the ▉▉▉ County Domestic Partnership Act of 1999;

5. We consent to this domestic partnership and said consent has not been obtained by force, duress, or fraud;

6. We agree to be jointly responsible for each other's basic food and shelter during our domestic partnership;

7. Neither of us has had a different domestic partner within the last thirty (30) days.

8. Our mailing addresses are:

Name _Robert_ ▉▉▉▉▉

Address ▉▉▉▉▉

City, State & Zip Code ▉▉▉▉▉

Name _Mark_ ▉▉▉▉▉

Address ▉▉▉▉▉

City, State & Zip Code ▉▉▉▉▉

Figure 1-9

Information Collected:

1. Establishment of relationship between two individuals.
2. When the domestic partnership was established (not shown in screenshot)
3. The address of both individuals

The image above shows the registered domestic partnership between two males. From this information we can infer about the target's sexual orientation which can lead to many negative consequences including losing a job (although illegal, some employers may create another reason) as well as violent hate crimes. This is one of the many documents posted on this website which also includes divorce, adoption and financial paperwork. This one website is just a sample of what is publicly searchable on the Internet.

The following images show one county's online tax bill pay system. Although this is a convenient way to pay taxes, having the ability to search by street address does not provide any type of verification that the information shown will be yours.

### Search Property Tax Information

Step 1 of 6

① ② ③ ④ ⑤ ⑥

This page allows you to search for ▮▮▮▮▮▮▮ secured, unsecured, and defaulted properties. Enter the desired mailing address, Assessor Parcel Number, or unsecured bill number to display a list of matching or related records.

**Search for property tax bills by Mailing Address . . .**

Street Address                    (optional)          Zip Code

[_____]  [Select Street Type ▼]  [_____]

▮▮▮▮▮▮▮▮▮▮▮▮

**Or search by Assessor Parcel Number, or by Supplemental bill number, or Escape bill number**

Bill Number: [_____] (10 digits with no dashes)

**Or search by unsecured bill number. . .**

Enter Tax Year (4 digits): [_____]   Bill Number (6 digits): [_____]

[ Begin Search ]

You can pay your property taxes by using credit card (VISA, Master Card) or echeck. There is no convenience fee for using echeck but a 1.88% fee is charged by credit card company. Click Go to find out how much your convenience fee will be.          [ Go ]

Figure 1-10

| | Bill No | Owner | Status | Min Due | Total Due | Specify Amount(s) to Pay |
|---|---|---|---|---|---|---|
| View Detail | 2005-80 | | DELINQUENT | 1180.97 | 1180.97 | See Bill Details |
| View Detail | 2006-00 | | DELINQUENT | 15.86 | 15.86 | Pay Total Due ☐ |
| View Detail | 2005-80 | | DELINQUENT | 583.69 | 583.69 | See Bill Details |
| View Detail | 2007-07 | | DELINQUENT | 127.47 | 127.47 | Pay Total Due ☐ |
| View Detail | 2009-01 | | DELINQUENT | 201.75 | 201.75 | Pay Total Due ☐ |
| View Detail | 2010-00 | | PAID | 0.00 | 0.00 | No Payment Due |

**Defaulted**

| | Parcel No | Owner | Status | Min Due | Total Due | Specify Amount(s) to Pay |
|---|---|---|---|---|---|---|
| View Detail | 541-280 | | DUE | 3456.66 | 3456.66 | Pay Total Due: ☐ |
| View Detail | 541-280 | | PAID | 0.00 | 0.00 | No Payment Due |
| View Detail | 541-280 | | PAID | 0.00 | 0.00 | No Payment Due |
| View Detail | 541-570 | | PAID | 0.00 | 0.00 | No Payment Due |

Figure 1-11

Information Collected:

1. Inference of person financial status
2. Property ownership

The information shown above included payments made on time as well as delinquent tax payments. Searching just a street name without numbers will produce these results. By doing this you can maximize your search on the individual property as well as find out who or what companies own properties around your target.

## Family Watch Dog

Family Watchdog is a national sex offender database. This website allows you to search for an individual by name or within a certain radius of an address. The website for this is http://www.familywatchdog.us.

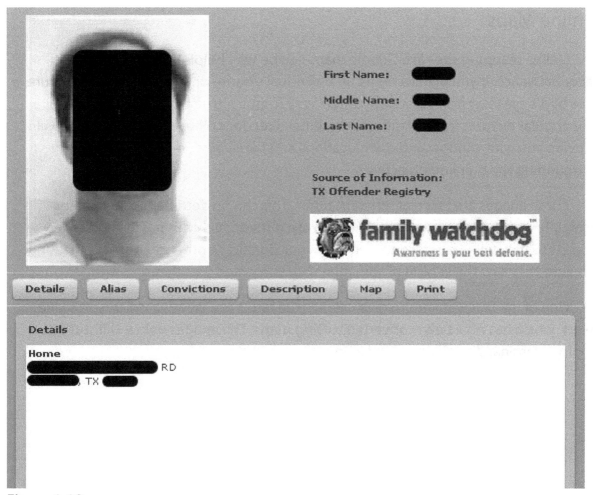

First Name:

Middle Name:

Last Name:

Source of Information:
TX Offender Registry

**family watchdog™**
Awareness is your best defense.

| Details | Alias | Convictions | Description | Map | Print |

Details

**Home**
RD
, TX

Figure 1-12

Information Collected:

1. Partial criminal record including offense (detailed in "Description")
2. Home address
3. Possible work Address
4. Possible convictions
5. Map of home address and also possibly work address
6. Photograph of target

The results include the offender's home address as an awareness measure.

# Online Maps

Online mapping sites like Google maps can be very helpful when it comes to reconnaissance. If you plan to target an individual's house or any man made structure, a true bird's eye view from a satellite can be very useful. A true bird's eye view will give you angular pictures from all different cardinal directions. These different angles will provide you with window and door locations and familiarize you with the land surrounding the building objective.

These images are taken at different times. This can be detrimental or it can be useful. To use it to your advantage you can see different vehicles parked and other objects to help with your recon. Imagine if your significant other caught you cheating because they saw the vehicle of someone they suspected you cheating with.

One of the first websites to give users a true bird's eye view was Microsoft's Live maps, which has now been converted to Bing maps. The images below will show you the four cardinal directions around a house.

Figure 1-13

Figure 1-1

Figure 1-15

Figure 1-16

Now that we've reconnoitered all sides of the houses, let's get a closer look at the front door with Google Street View.

Figure 1-17

Information Collected:

1. Type of house (Single level, Duplex in example)
2. Number of levels
3. Number, type, color of vehicles owned (rare but possible license plate number)
4. Entry/exit points (windows and doors)
5. Surrounding area

We have now completed an aerial and partial ground reconnaissance without even leaving our computers.

## Internet Archive

The Wayback Machine at archive.org provides historical snapshots and other archived data from around the Internet. According to Wikipedia, as of 2009 the Wayback Machine held 3 petabytes of data and is growing at a rate of 100 terabytes a month.

Although the Wayback Machine provides information that happened in the past, the data miner can use this historical information to their benefit. Information from an individual's past can help to determine the status of a person today. This information can be so useful in fact, that U.S. federal government agencies have requested information directly from the owners of Wayback Machine, Internet Archive. Below is a screen shot of an article about personal identifiable information being posted online. If this site had been archived, it would have been available much longer.

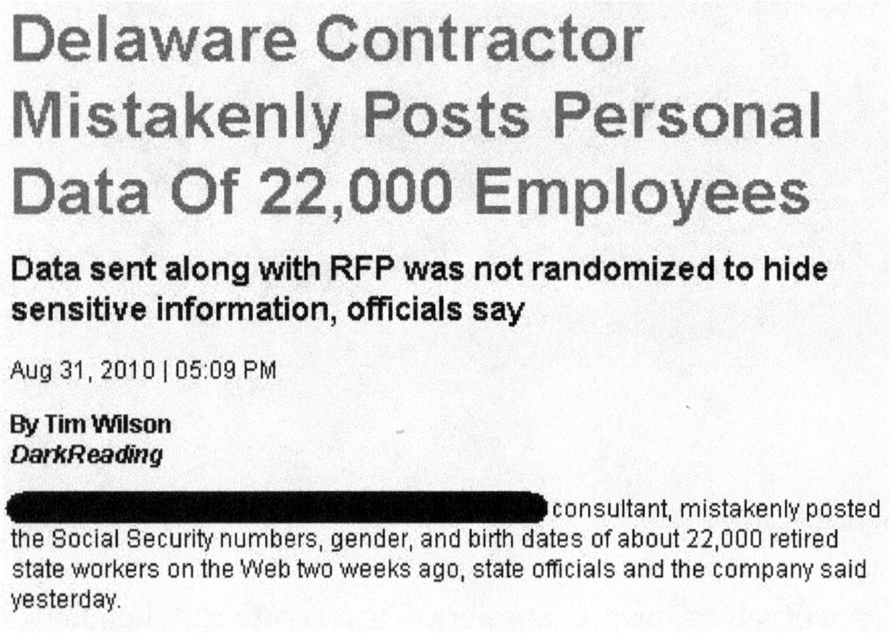

# Delaware Contractor Mistakenly Posts Personal Data Of 22,000 Employees

**Data sent along with RFP was not randomized to hide sensitive information, officials say**

Aug 31, 2010 | 05:09 PM

**By Tim Wilson**
*DarkReading*

██████████████████████ consultant, mistakenly posted the Social Security numbers, gender, and birth dates of about 22,000 retired state workers on the Web two weeks ago, state officials and the company said yesterday.

Figure 1-18

## Peer-to-Peer Software

Peer-to-Peer (P2P) computer software became popular around 2000 with the music sharing application Napster. With this program you could share music with anyone else who was also using the application. Since then P2P applications have become plentiful and have expanded their file sharing capabilities to almost any type of file including videos, pictures and even PDF and Microsoft Word documents.

The problem with these applications is that some users do not know how to properly configure them. Instead of sharing only the folders containing media such as music and movies, inexperienced users will end up sharing a part of their hard drive they do not wish others to see or sometimes even the entire hard drive itself! As we know all to well sharing your entire hard drive could expose personal information such as the images shown below.

| | Name | Type |
|---|---|---|
| | Black Eyed Peas – Boom Boom Pow | mp3 |
| | Rise Against – Injection | mp3 |
| | Martina Mcbride – In My Daughters Eyes | mp3 |
| | Black Eyed Peas – Meet me half way | mp3 |

Figure 1-19

Information Collected:

1. Music preferences

| | Name | Type | Size |
|---|---|---|---|
| | The Simpsons Movie | mpg | 224.3 MB |
| | -Loose Change – A Documentary on 911 Part 1 | mpg | 46.8 MB |
| | The Family Guy Movie | mp4 | 196.9 MB |
| | Harry Potter And The Order Of The Phoenix (2007) | mpg | 787.8 MB |
| | The Simpsons – Chili Cook Off | mpg | 202.7 MB |
| | Loose Change – A Documentary on 911 Part 2 | mpg | 46.8 MB |
| | The Simpsons Harry Potter spoof. | mpg | 224.8 MB |
| | The Simpsons – Crayon in Brain | mpg | 217.7 MB |

Figure 1-20

Information Collected:

1. Video entertainment preferences

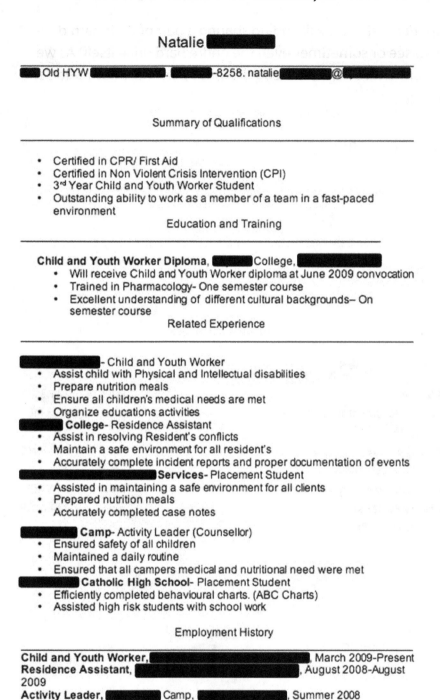

# Natalie ▮▮▮▮▮▮

▮▮ Old HYW ▮▮▮▮▮▮. ▮▮▮-8258. natalie▮▮▮▮▮@▮▮▮▮

## Summary of Qualifications

- Certified in CPR/ First Aid
- Certified in Non Violent Crisis Intervention (CPI)
- 3rd Year Child and Youth Worker Student
- Outstanding ability to work as a member of a team in a fast-paced environment

## Education and Training

**Child and Youth Worker Diploma,** ▮▮▮ College, ▮▮▮▮▮▮
- Will receive Child and Youth Worker diploma at June 2009 convocation
- Trained in Pharmacology- One semester course
- Excellent understanding of different cultural backgrounds– On semester course

## Related Experience

▮▮▮▮▮- Child and Youth Worker
- Assist child with Physical and Intellectual disabilities
- Prepare nutrition meals
- Ensure all children's medical needs are met
- Organize educations activities

▮▮▮ **College**- Residence Assistant
- Assist in resolving Resident's conflicts
- Maintain a safe environment for all resident's
- Accurately complete incident reports and proper documentation of events

▮▮▮▮▮**Services**- Placement Student
- Assisted in maintaining a safe environment for all clients
- Prepared nutrition meals
- Accurately completed case notes

▮▮▮ **Camp**- Activity Leader (Counsellor)
- Ensured safety of all children
- Maintained a daily routine
- Ensured that all campers medical and nutritional need were met

▮▮▮ **Catholic High School**- Placement Student
- Efficiently completed behavioural charts. (ABC Charts)
- Assisted high risk students with school work

## Employment History

**Child and Youth Worker,** ▮▮▮▮▮▮, March 2009-Present
**Residence Assistant,** ▮▮▮▮▮▮, August 2008-August 2009
**Activity Leader,** ▮▮▮ Camp, ▮▮▮▮, Summer 2008

Figure 1-21

Information Collected:

1.  Target's full name/address/phone number/email
2.  Resume (discussed in "Resumes and Professional" section)
3.  Religion (This individual attended a Catholic High School)

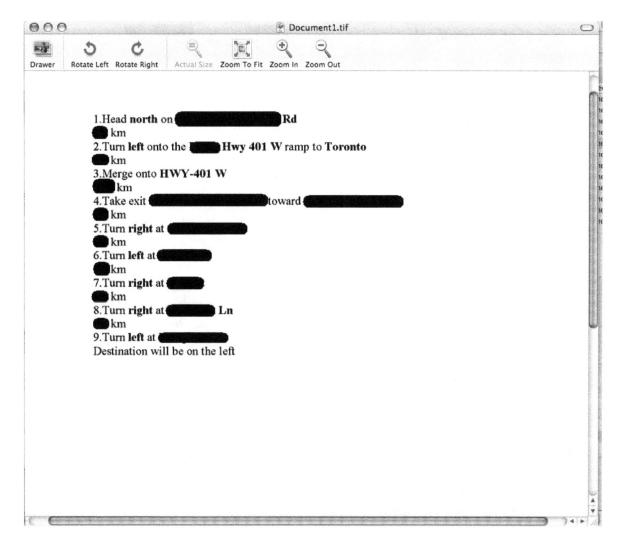

Figure 1-22

Information Collected:

1.  Possible location of someone connected to target

A quick Google search of these directions shows a residential area and will take you directly to within a few houses possible for the destination of these directions. A Google Street View is also available.

**Account Summary by Term**

5███████31 Natalie ████████
Sep 12, 2008 02:41 pm

This is your account summary by term. Anticipated third party contract payments, financial aid, and memos are **NOT** included in the summary.

Summary

| | |
|---|---|
| **Account Balance:** | $848.90 |

**Fall 2008**

| Description | Charge | Payment | Balance |
|---|---|---|---|
| Anc Fees Non T2202A Eligible | $75.00 | | $75.00 |
| Anc Fees T2202A Eligible | $341.50 | | $341.50 |
| Deferral Fees | $50.00 | | $0.00 |
| Residence Student Rent | $2,494.00 | | $2,494.00 |
| Res Application Fee | $20.00 | | $0.00 |
| Residence Deferral Fee | $100.00 | | $0.00 |
| Full-Time P.S. Tuition Fee | $1,050.40 | | $1,050.40 |
| OSAP - Financial Aid | | $3,112.00 | -$3,112.00 |
| Cash | | $20.00 | $0.00 |
| Visa | | $150.00 | $0.00 |
| **Term Charges:** | $4,130.90 | | |
| **Term Credits and Payments:** | $3,282.00 | | |
| **Term Balance:** | $848.90 | | |

**Winter 2008**

Figure 1-23

Information Collected:

1. Full name
2. University name (not shown in image)
3. Student account number
4. University costs and fees
5. Account balance

I wonder what the account number of the Visa credit card is she is using to pay? Probably this one:

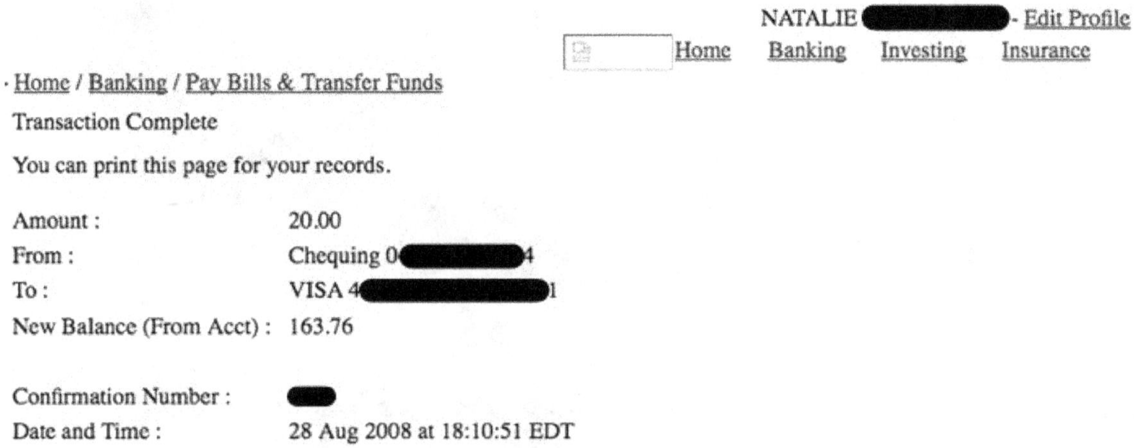

NATALIE ██████████ - Edit Profile

           Home   Banking   Investing   Insurance

· Home / Banking / Pay Bills & Transfer Funds

Transaction Complete

You can print this page for your records.

| | |
|---|---|
| Amount : | 20.00 |
| From : | Chequing 0█████████4 |
| To : | VISA 4█████████████1 |
| New Balance (From Acct) : | 163.76 |

| | |
|---|---|
| Confirmation Number : | ████ |
| Date and Time : | 28 Aug 2008 at 18:10:51 EDT |

Figure 1-24

Information Collected:

1. Full name
2. Bank name (easy to find a routing number)
3. Checking account number
4. Visa credit card number

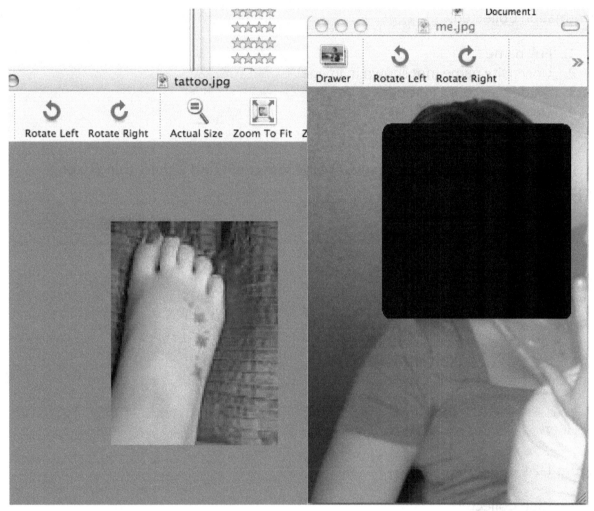

Figure 1-25

Information Collected:

1. Photograph of target appropriately labeled "me.jpg"
2. Identifying mark (tattoo)

## Social Networking

Since social networking sites are covered ad nauseam in other books and aspects of the media, we will only touch upon the subject here. The point of social networking sites such as Facebook and Twitter is to communicate and create a network of friends. Part of those two objectives is to share information and link profiles.

The screenshot below is a blatant example of a user giving away too much information.

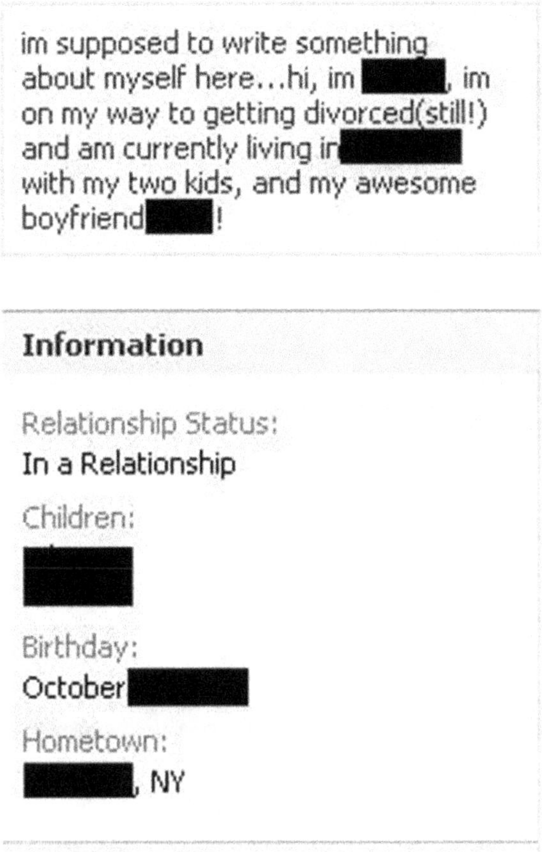

im supposed to write something about myself here...hi, im ███████, im on my way to getting divorced(still!) and am currently living in ████████ with my two kids, and my awesome boyfriend ████!

**Information**

Relationship Status:
In a Relationship

Children:
████████

Birthday:
October ████████

Hometown:
████████, NY

Figure 1-26

An example of linking Facebook profiles would be when you accept a friend request. This means that others users can now see that these two people have some type of connection with each other. Another example of linking profiles is when two people are dating they must request that the other accept the change in relationship status. Once this occurs, information is shown on the users Facebook profile that they are "in a relationship"/"Married"/etc with the other person. This concept also works with parents and siblings as you can see below:

**About Me**

Basic Info          Sex:                Female
                    Birthday:           January ▮

                    Parents:            Jane ▮▮▮▮▮
                                        Rick ▮▮▮▮

                    Siblings:           ▮▮▮▮▮
                                        Daniel ▮▮▮
                                        Katie ▮▮▮
                    Relationship        In a Relationship with ▮▮▮▮▮▮
                    Status:

                    Interested In:      Men
                    Looking For:        Friendship

                    Current City:       ▮▮▮▮ New York
                    Hometown:           ▮▮▮ New York
                    Political Views:    Liberal

Figure 1-27

Information Collected:

1. Target's significant other
2. Partial family tree of target
3. Political views
4. Sexual orientation
5. Birthday
6. Current location
7. What the target considers their "hometown"

Not only are you only able to get information about who the target is dating or married to, but you now may be able to double your information on the target. If your target is smart enough and blocks information and pictures from being seen by the public, it may still show who they are in a relationship with. If you are lucky enough to see this information, you can simply click on the significant other's name. If they allow their profile to be seen by the public, you will probably now have multiple pictures of your target. (Who doesn't take pictures with their significant other?)

Also, if a target shares their pictures to the public, lots of information can be collected this way. Location, hobbies and activities, place of employment, entertainment interests, educational institution and much more can be collected just by analyzing photographs of the target. Also, be mindful of the background in pictures. Many individuals will only concentrate on the foreground of pictures while being oblivious to the background. A humorous example of this is about a well-known picture of an individual selling a kettle on an Australian online auction site.

Figure 1-28

The nude man in this photograph posted this picture online only concentrating on the kettle itself and not the reflection in the kettle.

Another social networking site, Twitter, is a website where users can post short updates. Twitter is essentially a blog but allows a user only 140 characters per posting. By default, Twitter allows postings to be publicly viewable.

Many things can be revealed and inferred about a target through their blog postings and Facebook/Twitter updates. A short list could be a user's locations, current activities, relationship issues and political stance.

## Defense

You can regulate much of your personal information on the Internet. This theme is followed throughout the book as many people give away information freely without considering the possible consequences. Take into consideration the following websites and other software:

1.      Amazon.com Wishlist
2.      Facebook, Myspace, Twitter, etc
3.      Careerbuilder, Monster, LinkedIn
4.      Peer-to-peer software

You can choose to use the above websites and software, how much information you share with the world, or decide not to use them at all. If your employer posts information about you on their websites, simply ask them to remove it. If they refuse to remove your information, consult your lawyer.

Although the above websites are easy to deal with, others may not be. Websites such as Classmates.com and public record websites are more difficult to remove your information from. You should be able to contact these websites (or a lawyer) to inquire as to how you can remove your information from their database.

You should also be aware of geo tagging. Geo tagging is a process in which geographical information is embedded into the photos you take with a camera or camera phone. When posting these images online, the information can be extracted from these photos thereby placing you at certain places at certain times.

# 2

# AUTOMATED SEARCH TOOLS AND SERVICES

Although this chapter could be filed under Chapter 1, "Internet," it is quite different. Whereas Chapter 1 focused on the collector harvesting the information from different sites and sources, this chapter features specific websites that are more automated for the very purpose of collecting information. This chapter will include a section on the Google search engine. Google is featured here because of its power search engine that allows users to use formulas. We will only cover certain formulas that can be used as Johnny Long has covered the topic of "Google Hacking" in his series for Syngress Publishing.

## ZabaSearch

ZabaSearch is a website that acts like a phone book with more functionality and information. As you can see from the screen shot below ZabaSearch markets itself as a "Public Information Search Engine."

# **ZABA**SEARCH

**Free People Search and Public Information Search Engine**

**People Search by Name.** i.e. *john doe* or *john a doe*

[                                              ]

[ All 50 States ∨ ] [ Free People Search ]

**Search by Phone Number**. i.e. *555-555-5555*

[                  ] [ Search by Phone Number ]

**Telephone Numbers and Addresses Revealed Free. No Registration Required. Instant Results.**
**Three Times More Residential Listings than White Pages Phone Directory**
Other people finders still charge for information available here free.

Premium Services: Search by Phone Number  Search by SS#  Run a Background Check

Figure 2-1

By searching for a name you can find a variety of results. Including a state helps keep the returned information slim but is not required. The results below are returned with a basic name search.

Figure 2-2

Information Collected:

1. Address of target
2. Phone number of target
3. Birth year of target

Many of these results are the same individual and we can start to connect them after clicking on the name and displaying further results about the individual. For example, after selecting the name "Alex" with the phone number "-7545," it will display an address. This is the same address as the top result, "Alex" who lives in California on "Ave." The only other additional information shown by clicking on a result link will show an aerial view of the residence as shown in Chapter 1.

# Criminal Records

Although criminal records check services are plentiful on the Internet, rarely are the websites free. The website www.criminalsearches.com provides a database that anyone can search for free. Although the information can be useful if found, if a name does not show in the database do not assume they do not have a criminal background. This website is still in Beta and does not yet have a full database.

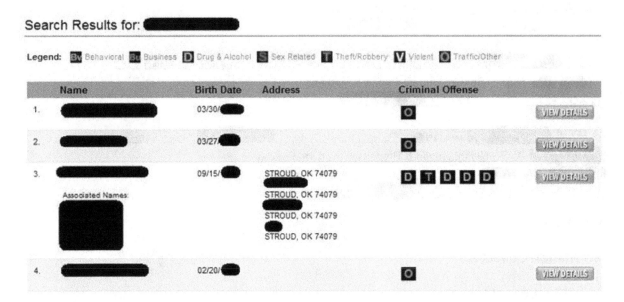

Figure 2-3

Information Collected:

1. Name/Aliases
2. Date of Birth
3. Violations

After selecting "View Details" the page in Figure 2-4 is displayed. This individual had 26 violations that could not be captured with a screen shot. All 26 violations were listed with limited details for each violation.

**SOURCE OF INFORMATION**

Oklahoma Department of Corrections Website, OK (more info...)

Oklahoma District Courts, OK (more info...)

OK Payne District Court, OK (more info...)

Ok District Court, OK (more info...)

**PERSONAL INFORMATION**

Full Name: ███████████     Date of Birth: ███████

AKAs: ███████████

Height: ███████████

Weight:

Hair Color:

Eye Color:

Race:

Gender:

**ADDRESSES**

Possible Previous Address 1: ████████

Possible Previous Address 2: █████████████

Possible Previous Address 3: █████████████

Possible Previous Address 4: ████████████

**CRIMINAL OFFENSE 1**

Offense Date:

Case Number: 041-TRC ██████

Offense Type: Traffic/Other

Offense Code:

Offense Description: FAILURE TO WEAR SAFETY BELT

Conviction Place: LINCOLN

Date Reported: 06/24/2003

Disposition: GUILTY PLEA

Figure 2-4

Information Collected:

1. Name/Alias/Date of Birth
2. Physical description

39

3. "Possible" address history
4. Detailed offenses

Although this website may still be adding names to the database, it has some other great features that may be worth taking a look at from a defensive point of view. The Neighborhood Watch feature can search for criminals within a certain radius of an address. With the Criminal Alerts option, it can alert you on the activities of up to 5 individuals. Although the Criminal Alerts feature is meant to be defensive, you can easily sign up and trace the activities of your target if they happen to become entangled in the legal system once again.

## Intelius

While using Zabasearch, many times it will provide a direct link to Intelius so that you may gather more information on the individual you are researching. This site can provide you with different levels of reportable information depending on how much you are willing to pay. In the sample report below you can see the types of information that are available via the Intelius service.

# Background Report

**Your Report:**

Overview ▶

Personal Public ▶
Records Data

Address History ▶

Property History ▶
Summary

Single State ▶
Criminal Check

Single State Civil ▶
Judgments

People Search ▶
Report

Marriage And ▶
Divorce Records

Death Records ▶

**Your Search:**

Name: ████████

Aliases: 1) ████████
2) ████████

Age: ████

**In This Report**

- Overview
- Personal Public Records Data
- Address History
- Property History Summary
- Single State Criminal Check
- Single State Civil Judgments
- People Search Report
- Marriage and Divorce Records
- Death Records

Figure 2-5

Information Collected:

1. Name/Aliases/personal information
2. Personal public records
3. Address history
4. Property History
5. Criminal records
6. Civil court judgments
7. Marriage/Divorce records
8. Death records

As you can see, this site can provide you with a vast amount of information on the target, of course depending on how much you are willing to pay for it. This website can also be a great resource for those hiring a personal assistant or a nanny for their children. No matter what type of information you are looking for, Intelius reports aren't that expensive (depending on your motivation) and usually yield some valuable information.

NOTE: Due to privacy laws in the United States, make sure you obtain a potential employee's authorization in writing before doing a background check.

## People Search Sites

Some websites on the Internet are specifically designed to search automatically for people. These sites crawl and search other databases for information and display all the results onto one page. There are countless numbers of them but we will focus on just two.

### Pipl.com

Pipl is a website where an individual can type the name, email, phone number or even a username of a target to gather more information about them. You can also search by business name. A simple name search will yield numerous results. Pipl breaks down the information into sections for organizational purposes, which help if you are targeting specific information. Besides just collecting information from other databases, Pipl displays "Quick Facts" which shows information from lesser-known websites. If your target had a write up in the local newspaper or played basketball for their university, those results would be displayed also.

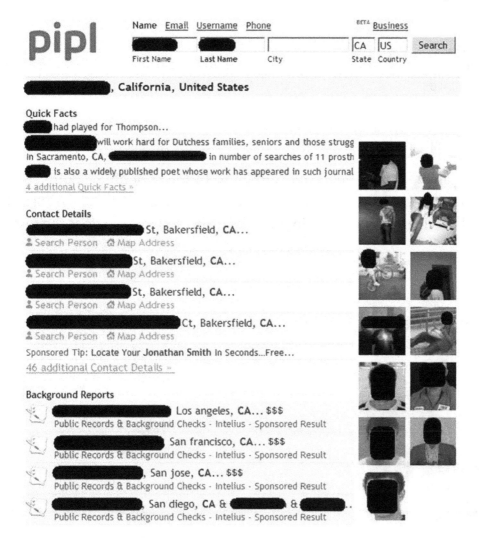

Figure 2-6

Information Collected:

1. Quick facts
2. Picture of Target
3. Contact Details
4. Personal Profiles
5. Schools and Classmates
6. Business profiles
7. Email Addresses

8. Videos
9. Publications
10. Public Records
11. Archived Records

## Spokeo

In addition to searching for someone by name, email address or phone number, Spokeo has a feature that allows you to directly connect to your email's address . Simply click on your email provider, provide your login information and Spokeo does the rest.

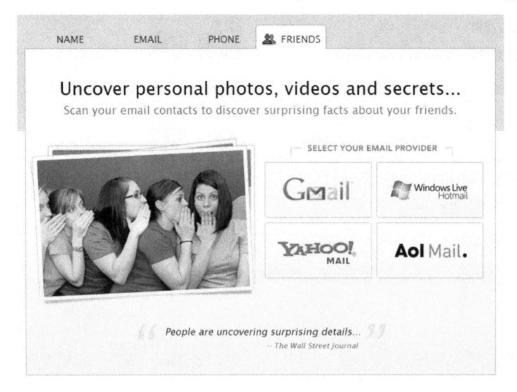

Figure 2-7

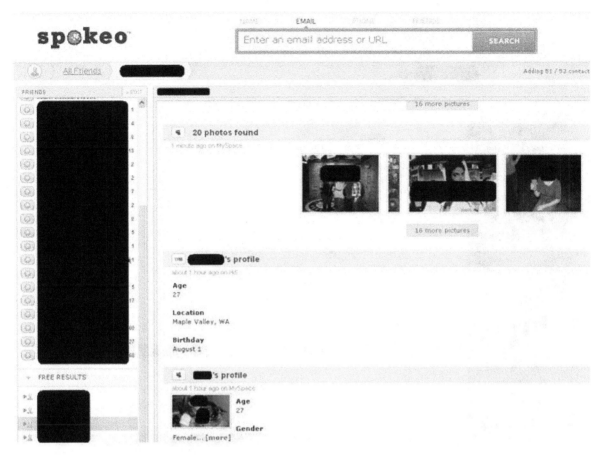

Figure 2-8

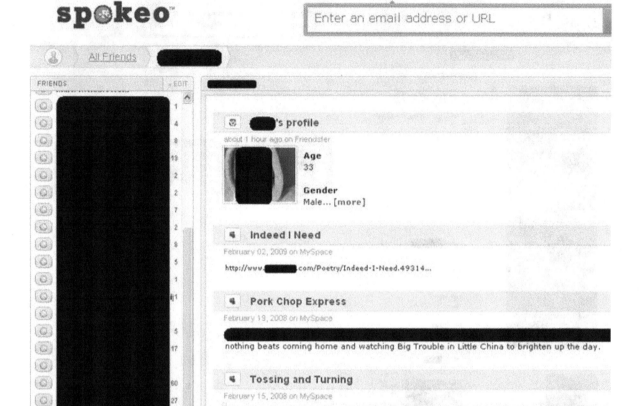

Figure 2-9

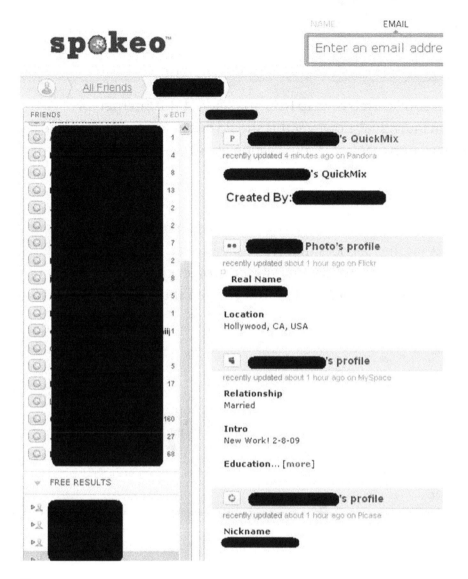

Figure 2-10

Information Collected:

1. Age/Sex/Location
2. Birthday
3. Photo of target
4. Blog entries
5. Music preference
6. Social Media profiles

7.  Relationship status
8.  Education
9.  Nickname

Many websites like Pipl and Spokeo exist to help you harvest the Internet for personal information on an individual; however this should not be your only resource if you wish to gather the maximum amount of information about your target.

## I.C.U. Inc.

I.C.U. Inc. can be found at www.tracerservivces.com and is an online private investigating website. I.C.U. Inc. has services that are so invasive and revealing that former President George W. Bush enacted several laws to protect citizens from the leakage of powerfully private information. The following screen shot is a list of services offered by I.C.U. Inc..

| | |
|---|---|
| Address Tracer | Marriage/Divorce Tracer |
| Address Verification | Motor Vehicle Tracer |
| Aircraft Tracer | National Business Tracer |
| Auto Title Tracer | Offshore Bank Account Tracer |
| Bank Account Tracer | Pager Cloning |
| Bankruptcy Tracer | Pager Records |
| Business Credit Report | P.O. Box Tracer |
| Business Type Tracer | Previous Employer Verification |
| Caller Identification | Prisoner Tracer |
| Canadian Bank Account Tracer | Professional License Verification |
| Cellular Phone Locater | Real estate Tracer |
| Change Of Address Tracer | SEC Annual Financial Report |
| Civil Suit Tracer | SEC Corporate Profile |
| Criminal History Check | Social Security Number Developer |
| Complete Asset Search | Social Security Number Tracer |
| Complete Business Asset Search | Stocks & Bonds Tracer |
| Corporation Tracer | Surname Listing Service |
| Credit Reports | Telephone Calling Card Spy |
| Current Employer Tracer | Telephone Number Tracer |
| Dead Beat Parent Asset Search | Telephone Toll Records |
| Driving Record Check | UCC Filing Tracer |
| Education Tracer | Unpublished Phone Numbers |
| Employer ID Number Developer | Utility Company Tracer |
| Human Tracer | VIN Verification |
| Key Codes Tracer | Welfare Tracer |
| License Plate Tracer | Workers Compensation Tracer |
| Marine Vehicle Tracer | |

Figure 2-11

As mentioned, some of the above services are no longer available due to federal law. However, that is only because I.C.U. Inc. follows U.S. law and will not process these requests. It does not mean that it can no longer be done and in terms of defense, it should still be considered a concern.

## Defense

Not much can be offered in the ways of defense in regards to this chapter. The sites mentioned often do not store the information in its own databases. Instead, they harvest other databases in order to serve the information on its own website. The best way to try and hunt down the source of the information would be to contact these websites and ask where they get the information and how you can go about removing it.

Other websites are simply public record. If you want to stay out of criminal records searches, don't be a criminal.

# 3

# THE GOOG

Whether it is the search engine or some other application it has developed such as Gmail, the Chrome web browser, and even cell phone operating systems and applications, Google is now a part of our everyday lives. Because Google has built in special codes and formulas the user can use in a search, it has become easier for us to find information. Johnny Long has perfected this art and has released two books on Google Hacking and maintains a database of codes at http://www.hackersforcharity.org/ghdb/.

Many readers may see this chapter as too technical however the multitude of chapters specifically dealing with Internet sources proves how we have come to rely on computers and the Internet, especially for the sharing of information. If you are technically inept, please continue to read this chapter. It will show you the capabilities those who are technically proficient have and make you aware of the dangers of sharing too much information.

## Open Webcams

Although sharing how to access web cameras with Google (or any other information in this chapter) is beyond the scope of this book and is better addressed in the "Google Hacking for Penetration Testers" series of books from Syngress Publishing, the fact is that it is possible. I will show examples of some webcams that I found with a simple Google search. Some of these cameras aren't intended for viewing by individuals outside the company/school/family/etc but they are. We will analyze why giving others access to these cameras can give away information.

Figure 3-1

From the translation of the text in the upper left corner, it seems this camera may have been put up to spy on a neighbor. This helps emphasize the point this book is trying to make. Perhaps the target was to engage in some illegal activity? Perhaps the target was cheating on their spouse? This could cause all types of privacy and legal issues.

Plenty of scenarios can be concocted from the image and reason why the camera was placed in this position. Once again, the point of this image is that it is possible.

Figure 3-2

The web camera above is all too common. This one seems to be a student computer lab at a university. The problem with cameras such as these is that they have a clear view of monitors and keyboards, which doesn't allow for much privacy. If the two nearest workspaces had been occupied, we would have been able to view what the target was doing on the computer including private emails, student grades and logging into bank accounts. With the addition of the clear view of the keyboard, we would have been easily able to shoulder surf, or watch a target type in their usernames and passwords to any website they visited.

Figure 3-3

This screenshot makes me laugh. Not only because they decided to focus on a clock with a drinking bird, but also because this company is in the "video security" industry. This company thought it would be clever to put a clock and a drinking bird in front of a camera, however they completely overlooked the computer monitor in full view and the open shades in the background.

With the shades open, the general public can observe company activities in the hallway. Although it may not seem like much, information can be gleaned from body language alone. How would you as a stalking victim feel if you knew that you were being watched in the hallways at work? The computer could be used for processing client information. When providing security for others, giving away this type of information freely on the Internet is downright incompetent.

Many of the above web cameras have the ability for the public user to take over control. This means that you can move the camera from left to right and up and down, and better yet, zoom. Zooming the camera makes it a lot easier to watch activities on monitors and target's entering passwords. Also, many extra-marital affairs happen in offices. If a target were caught, blackmail would be very simple.

## Open Printers

Many printers today come with hard drives installed so they can handle larger documents and larger quantities of documents. They are also usually connected to the company's network and subsequently the Internet. With some crafty Google searches, we can view the print queue on some of these printers.

| ID | Job Name | Owner | Host Name | Output Result | Impression Number | No. of Sheets | Host I/F | Job Submitted Time |
|---|---|---|---|---|---|---|---|---|
| 19064 | Microsoft Word - Lewis Hall Renovations Naming Opportunities9.1 | b███ | 32118-LAW | Completed | 1 | 1 | LPD | 2010/10/12 13:52:26 |
| 19065 | Microsoft Word - Order of the Coif program2010EB.docx | b███ | 32118-LAW | Completed | 2 | 2 | LPD | 2010/10/12 14:00:55 |
| 19066 | Microsoft Office Outlook - Memo Style | t███ | 32120-LAW | Completed | 1 | 1 | LPD | 2010/10/12 17:34:14 |
| 19067 | GLJ-WL German Law in Context 2010 Program.pdf | p███ | 32098-LAW | Completed | 5 | 5 | LPD | 2010/10/13 09:38:45 |
| 19068 | http://mevexvc1.███edu/EnterpriseVault/ViewMessage.asp?Vaul | p███ | 32098-LAW | Completed | 2 | 2 | LPD | 2010/10/13 10:06:03 |
| 19069 | Law Advisory for Peter.pdf | p███ | 32098-LAW | Completed | 2 | 2 | LPD | 2010/10/13 14:07:01 |
| 19070 | Microsoft Word - hendricksspeaker.docx | p███ | 32098-LAW | Completed | 1 | 1 | LPD | 2010/10/14 10:39:04 |
| 19071 | Schedule_Automatic_Reports.pdf | LawTech | | Completed | 2 | 2 | LPD | 2010/10/14 11:12:00 |
| 19072 | RE: Applicant FAQ Email - For Yo | LawTech | | Completed | 2 | 2 | LPD | 2010/10/14 12:35:00 |
| 19073 | RE: Applicant FAQ Email - For Yo | LawTech | | Completed | 2 | 2 | LPD | 2010/10/14 13:50:00 |

Figure 3-4

I could write an entire chapter itself on the why having a printer open to the Internet is a bad idea but since this book is about privacy and information collection, let's take a look at the screen shot above.

First, we know that this printer belongs to a university and which university it belongs to because of the URL showing as the job name.

Second, it looks like Lewis Hall is being renovated and it may involve renovations to its name as well. What if the university does not want it to be publicly known that planned renovations will take place?

Third, there are other publicly accessible URLs in this print queue, cropped from the image above for privacy. If we copy and paste those URLs into a web browser, we can now see the documents this user printed. Also, because we also know the university's URL and the user name of the target who printed them, we can reasonably figure out the individuals name and search for his profile on the university's website (remember "Employer Websites" in Chapter 1).

In addition to this information, we also have access to how many pages the document was that was printed as well as a time stamp. The timestamp may help to show a person's location at a certain time.

## Open VoIP

Voice over Internet Protocol (VoIP) is becoming a very popular way to manage office phone systems. These systems usually require a central server to connect through the Internet, in some way, to place phone calls. Some operators do not properly secure their systems, unwillingly providing information about the clients or partners the target company does business with.

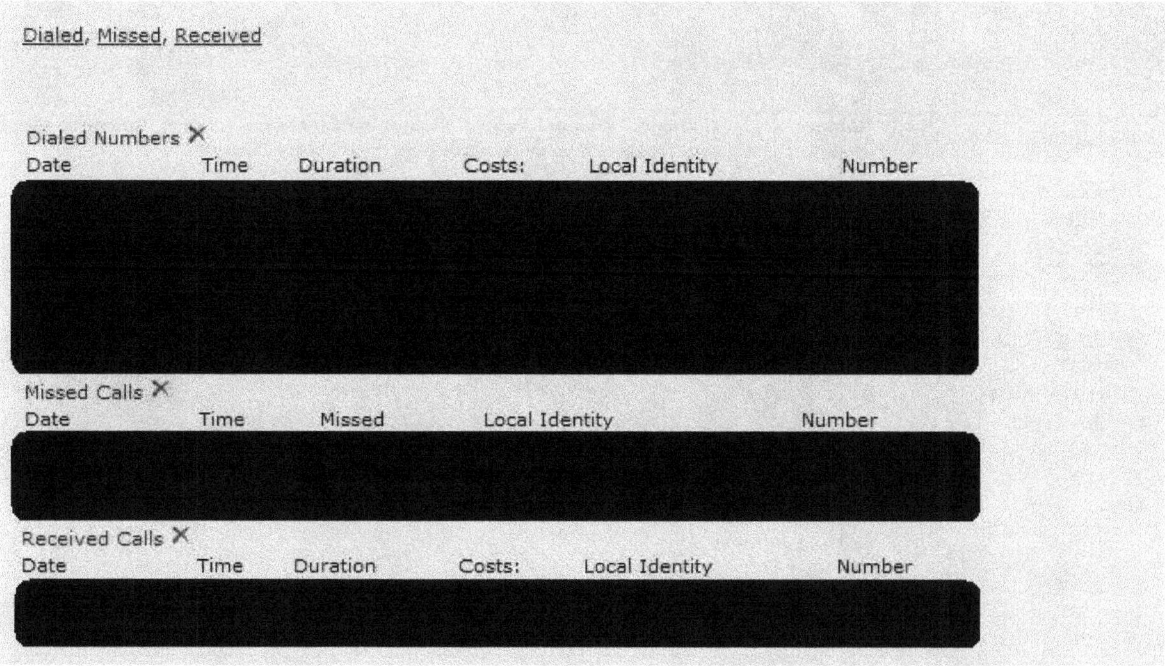

Dialed, Missed, Received

Dialed Numbers ✕

| Date | Time | Duration | Costs: | Local Identity | Number |
|------|------|----------|--------|----------------|--------|

Missed Calls ✕

| Date | Time | Missed | Local Identity | Number |
|------|------|--------|----------------|--------|

Received Calls ✕

| Date | Time | Duration | Costs: | Local Identity | Number |
|------|------|----------|--------|----------------|--------|

Figure 3-5

In the above screen shot, this VoIP system is displaying the phone number the target company has dialed, missed, and received. Additional information includes a time stamp and duration of the call. This information exposure can lead to a target association matrix, as explained in Chapter 1.

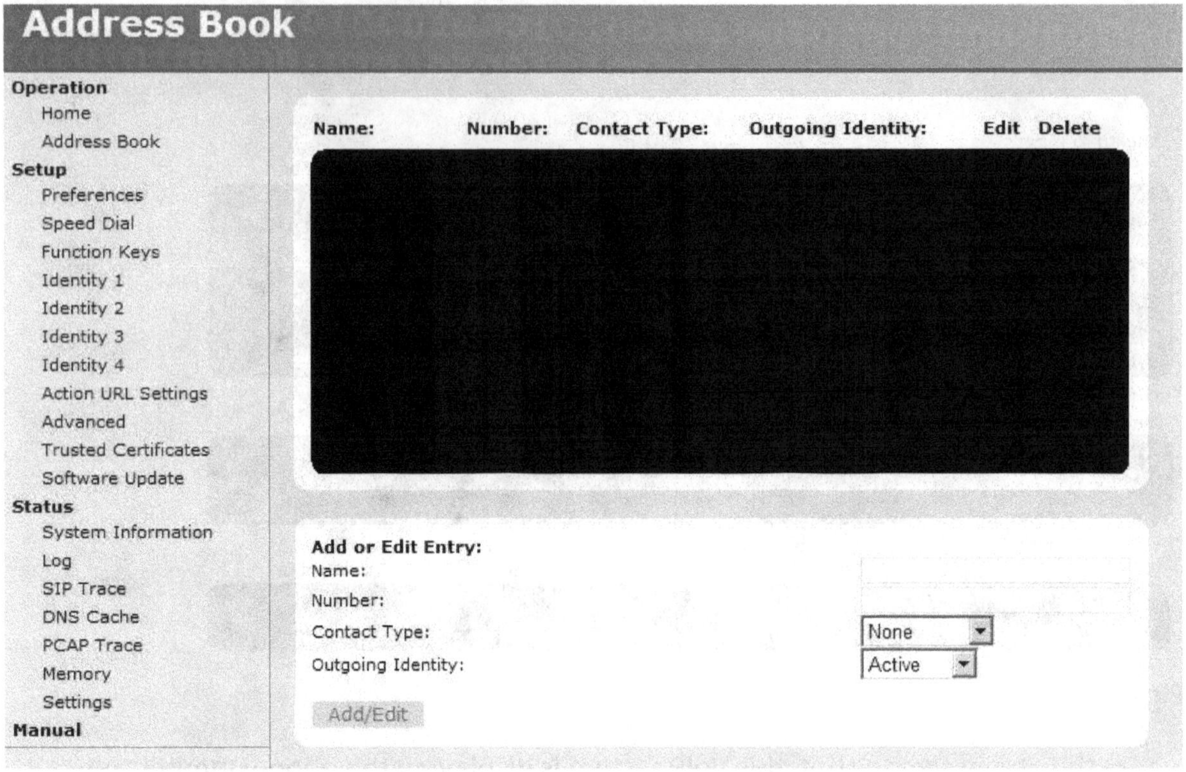

## Address Book

**Operation**
Home
Address Book
**Setup**
Preferences
Speed Dial
Function Keys
Identity 1
Identity 2
Identity 3
Identity 4
Action URL Settings
Advanced
Trusted Certificates
Software Update
**Status**
System Information
Log
SIP Trace
DNS Cache
PCAP Trace
Memory
Settings
**Manual**

| Name: | Number: | Contact Type: | Outgoing Identity: | Edit | Delete |
|-------|---------|---------------|--------------------|------|--------|

**Add or Edit Entry:**
Name:
Number:
Contact Type:                None
Outgoing Identity:           Active

Add/Edit

Figure 3-6

An address book is also a great way to form a target association matrix. The address book feature can be more beneficial because of the "Contact Type" column. Although this column was probably meant to be filled in whether the contact was personal or business related, some systems allow a user to type in whatever they wish. Because of this, a target may expose more information than they need to by identifying what company or what type of relative the phone number belongs to such a cousin, brother or parent.

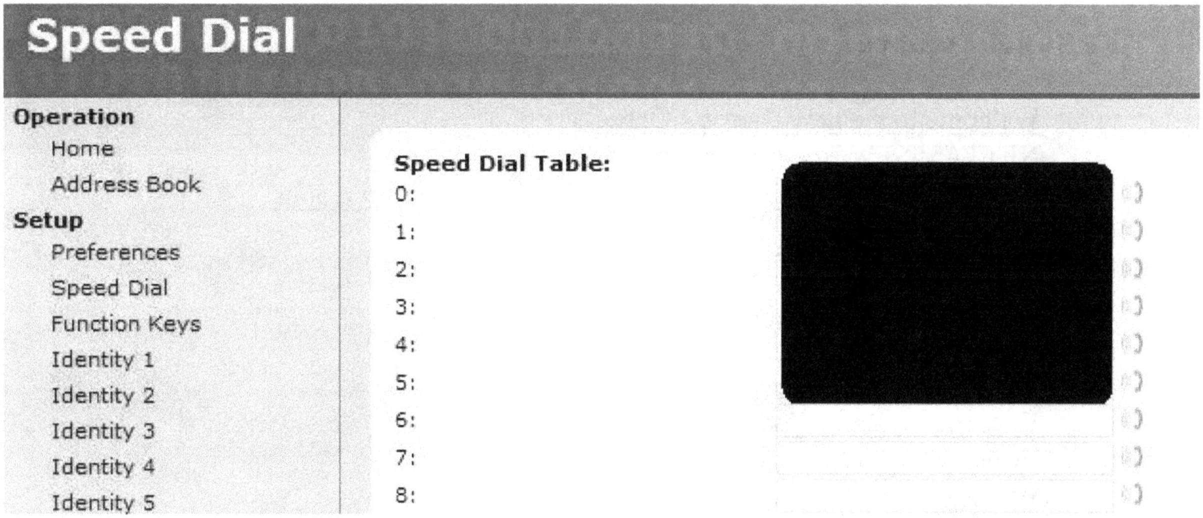

## Speed Dial

**Operation**
Home
Address Book
**Setup**
Preferences
Speed Dial
Function Keys
Identity 1
Identity 2
Identity 3
Identity 4
Identity 5

**Speed Dial Table:**
0:
1:
2:
3:
4:
5:
6:
7:
8:

Figure 3-7

With the information from the first two screen shots in this section, we can now use the speed dial information in the target association matrix. In combination with the dialed/missed/received calls information we can accurately determine who the target call and how often. We can use this in our association matrix by determining which phone numbers our target has stronger bonds with.

Phone numbers can yield a great deal of information about your target. Associations of your target can reveal other doors to which you can reach your target. If your target proves difficult when achieving your ultimate goal, your target's associates may be easier. As you gain the trust of your target's associates it will then be easier to gain the trust of your target.

## Internet Browser History and Bookmarks

When a person uses the Internet, typically they will only browse websites that are of interest to them. This is particularly true when bookmarking a site. By having a look at a target's web browser history or bookmarks, we can have insight into how they use the Internet. Besides the obvious interests and hobbies you will see in the screenshots below, we can also accurately deduce the target's political leanings and career choice, among other things.

## Personal Finance

Welcome to the new Barron's Online
NETTAVISEN Børstjenester
Foreign currencies and currency Exchange Rates history graphs
SKAGEN Fondene
Parat24
Lånekassens informasjonssider
Parat24
CGU Privelege Portfolio
Welcome to PaineWebber EDGE
Universal Fonds ASA
Welcome to PaineWebber EDGE
My Netscape
Money.com Portfolio Tracker
Money.com
Time Warner's Pathfinder!
Yahoo! Finance - World Markets
Yahoo! Finance
Finance Page for [Guest]
Gjensidige InternettBank
NETTAVISEN Børstjenester: Valuta
NETTAVISEN Børsindekser utland
NETTAVISEN Økonomi
NETTAVISEN
Salomon Smith Barney Access
PaineWebber - Investment Advice and Financial Services
Velkommen til Gjensidige InternettBank

Figure 3-8

## Facts/Data Resources

EarthTrends: The Environmental Information Portal
The World Bank Group--World Development Indicators - Environment
World Sites Atlas
CIA -- The World Factbook 2000 -- Country Listing
Search Results - world atlas
Earthscan Publications Home Page
CNN - World Time
CIA World Factbook 1998
Atlas of the World
Greenwich 2000: Time Channel
World time zone map with current local times all over the World

## Radio/News

Newsweek Front Page 10:14 PM ET Thursday, September 13, 2001
Dagbladet.no
dn.no
Guardian Unlimited | Special reports | George W Bush's America
This Week's Show
The New York Times on the Web
Klassekampen
CNN.com - Election 2000 - Results
ens
smh.com.au - The Sydney Morning Herald
Aftenposten Interaktiv
CNN.com
The Economist
New Scientist - News, jobs and more from the leading weekly science magazine
MSNBC Cover
CNBC Asia
Washingtonpost.com - News Front

Figure 3-9

## Conservation Stuff

RESOURCE LINKS
Conservation Ecology - A Peer Reviewed Journal - Main Page
The 2000 IUCN Red List of Threatened Species
Cat Specialist Group Home Page
NCBI Taxonomy Homepage
NLE Adds Search Capability to CRS Reports Database
The Unabomber Manifesto - Table Of Contents
Search Results - an ecologist lives in a world of wounds
Wilderness Defense!
Environmental Ethics: Values in and Duties to the Natural World
In Defense of All Life - "You cannot control what is wild"
Earth First! Worldwide
GLOBAL WITNESS HOME PAGE
Wilderness Defense! Deep Ecology
GEO-2000: Table of Contents
IUCN - The World Conservation Union - International Biodiversity Day 2001, May 22
IPCC reports
Centres of Plant Diversity: The Americas

Figure 3-10

## Marine Stuff

ICRI international coral reef initiative - english home page

## Forest stuff

Science -- Laurance et al. 291 (5503): 438
Forest Conservation Portal -- Rainforest, Forest and Biodiversity Conservation News & Information
Forest Conservation Links : Forest Protection : Environmental Campaigns
Sustainable Harvest of Non-timber Plant Resources
Ecoforestry Institute - Welcome to the future of forestry
Global Forest Watch Home Page
    CTYPE NETSCAPE-Bookmark-fil
    This is an automatically generated file.
    It will be read and overwritten.
    Do Not Edit!
    LE>Bookmarks for Allan Tarua</TI
E/CN.17/1997/12 Report of the Ad Hoc Intergovernmental Panel on Forests on its fourth session

## Population Stuff

World POPClock Projection
World Population
The Happiness Index. May 25, 2000. The Connection with Christopher Lydon.
VHEMT Links Page
Worldwatch Institute Home Page
CONSTRAINTS ON THE EXPANSION OF THE GLOBAL FOOD SUPPLY
Zero Population Growth
Population.com
Population Communications International
Country Briefing Books
Population and Environment Linkages Service
People & Planet

Figure 3-11

## Job stuff

The Communication Initiative - Vacancy, Recruitment - Vacancies Job Postings
Job Listings, Salaries, and Resume Tips
Current vacancies
Wildlife Conservation Society: Current Job Postings
The Leadership Development Programme
HotJobs.com
Monster.com
StepStone - Europe's leading online recruitment centre. Jobs updated daily
New Scientist Jobs
The Chronicle of Higher Education: Career Network
Monster.com - Work. Life. Possibilities.
Job Oppoturnities at UNESCO

## Princeton stuff

Princeton University Office of Career Services
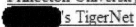's TigerNet

## PNG Stuff

PNGVILLAGE.COM - Ples Bilong PNG On The World Wide Web
The National Online
Post-Courier Online
Journalism UPNG: Directory
PNG Independent Online
Conservation Resource Centre - Papua New Guinea
Datec Papua New Guinea
PNG main
Papua New Guinea Virtual Library

## Norway stuff

Figure 3-12

## Fun stuff

Nobody expects the Spanish inquisition skit
ulvensvenner
The Correct Time and Moon Phase
Onepine Main template
Welcome to Carousel Kites Online
Kite Reviews - The Power Kite Site
Kite Fantastic - Kite Database - T
Leading Edge Kite Co.
Kite Fantastic
Park Wars: The Little Menace - a ©2MuchTime Ltd production 1999-2001
Official Darwin Awards
Welcome to the Doonesbury Electronic Town Hall
Welcome to the Dilbert Zone®
South Park For Mac Users
Abnormal South Park - Sounds
Smiley Faces
Free Clip Art Center - [ Main Page ]
CoolGraphics.com - The Gallery
Clips Ahoy! Clip Art - Free Original Clipart images, graphics requests welcome!
Clipart.Com
Glossary of Internet Acronyms and Expressions

## Boating Stuff

Bruktbørsen
Nautilus A/S
BoatPoint Search Results Page
Kirton Kayaks home page
EYB, Multicriteria Search

Figure 3-13

From the above screen shots we can determine the following things about our target:

From Figure 3-8 we can determine where and how our target managers their money. If we where interested in stealing the target's money, we would already have a great start.

The target is Norwegian. This is determined from the language and URLs of the banks (.no is used, instead of .com, which is the country code for Norway) and supplemented by the target's name (not shown in screenshots). The section heading "Norway Stuff" helps confirms this.

The target's job is a professor at Princeton University in the Earth Science department, most likely ecology. We know this because in the section "Princeton Stuff," TigerNet is a link to the faculty webmail. We can determine the target's specialty because of all the links about conservation and ecology as well as the link in the "Job Stuff" section entitled "New Scientist Jobs." A faculty search of the target's name on the Princeton website would confirm this.

Figure 3-13 shows some of the target's interests outside of work.

We can guess that the target's political leanings by making several generalizations. Although this is not a 100% accurate way to determine a target's viewpoints, the more data we compare, the higher accuracy we will have. We can say with probable accuracy that the target's political leanings are liberal. We can say this by comparing the news outlets of choice, the industry the target works in (academia) and the target's specialty. Although these are generalizations, they can help us determine a target's viewpoint.

We also know by viewing the links in the "Fun Stuff" section that the target likes South Park and owns an Apple computer. This helps to determine the target's likes and hobbies.

## Google Latitude

Google Latitude is a program for smart phones that allows other individuals to see your location. That sentence alone should immediately cause an alarm. Although Google gives privacy settings such as controlling who sees your location, what level of detail and the ability to turn the feature on and off, not everyone does this or is aware how to. The following screenshot is an example from CNET.com on what the feature looks like.

Figure 3-14

Google Latitude can also log your location history and create alerts when friends are in a certain area.

To utilize this type of information on a target, if they don't have this feature set up already, you can introduce them to it or even install it on the target's phone without their knowledge. By doing this, you now have your own GPS tracker, a toy which even law enforcement is limited to use. You can now track your target's location and possibly analyze what they are doing at that certain time. For example, if your target is located at a restaurant around dinnertime, they are most likely not alone. More often than not, people go to dinner at restaurants with other individuals. Another use of Google Latitude to track your target would be to set alerts on your phone for when your target is in a certain area. The possibilities are endless and very useful for tracking if the situation is right.

## Defense

There are few ways to restrict Google from obtaining information about you. The first defense is simply to not create ways for Google's web crawler to find you. Do not use programs like Google Latitude or upload your bookmarks to web servers.

Another defense is to use a robots.txt file on your webpage. A robots.txt file is a file that a web crawler, like Google, reads to determine whether or not to index your web page in their database. You can search the Internet on how to implement a robots.txt file. However, to disallow web crawlers from indexing anything on your webpage you need the following:

User-agent: *
Disallow: /

Lastly, if you do find your information already indexed in Google's database, you can use the following URL to request removal:

https://www.google.com/webmasters/tools/removals

# 4

# HUMAN INTERACTION

Interacting with other humans can take many forms as we use a combination of our five senses to collect information. In this chapter, we will take a look at different ways you may be able to collect information about your target simply by interacting with other individuals or even the target themselves.

## Elicitation

Elicitation can simply be described as extracting information from an individual through social interaction, most commonly through conversation. Elicitation is not achieved by asking straightforward questions but rather guiding the conversation so the target is unaware you are collecting specific information about them.

One of the best examples of elicitation is in the movie The Wedding Singer with Adam Sandler. In this scene, Sandler's character is left alone with Drew Barrymore's character's fiancé after Barrymore and her sister leave for the bathroom. Sandler's character is able to extract information from Barrymore's fiancé about his recent infidelity. Sandler does this by simply pretending to be interested in the conversation and agreeing with the situation.

Sandler accomplishes tactful elicitation by employing two basic techniques. One is by showing disbelief and the other is by showing interest. If your target is simply telling you he robbed a bank and you feign disbelief, human nature tells your target to defend himself and to prove you wrong. In doing so your target will most likely tell you in detail how they managed to successfully rob a bank.

Human nature also helps when using the interest approach. If your target loves to talk about a certain subject, they tend to reveal more than they should. For example, if your subject is proud of their job, let's say military service, they may break operational security guidelines without even realizing it. If they start talking about their military service and you fake interest by saying "Really? That's impressive," your subject may start to open up and reveal more information now that they have found someone that will listen to them.

Falling victim to elicitation works in much the same way as falling victim to a social engineering attack (explained in Chapter 6). It comes down to several traits of human nature reactions and feelings. It is human nature to be helpful and polite to others. By doing this, a person's guard may be down they may end up interacting with others a little more than they should.

Another way we fall victim is because we all want to appear intelligent, especially about certain areas such as our jobs. The more someone talks to us about these subjects, the more we want to prove how much we know about it and relating it to our own lives.

Because humans are, by default, nice, helpful, and pleasant people, we are more reluctant to believe that others may want to use our information for nefarious reasons.

Sometimes you may not want to interact directly with your target for various reasons such as if they may recognize you. Besides sending a member of the opposite sex to extract information from your target, you can also interact with friends or acquaintances of your target. Your target's friends are less likely to know who you are in the relation to the target and the chances of suspicion are greatly reduced since you are collecting information about your target and not the friend themselves. A person is much more comfortable revealing information about someone else than they are of themselves.

# Body Language

The full concept and spectrum of body language is way beyond the scope of this book, as plenty of books have already been written on the subject. Body language, however, is one of the most common, nonverbal ways to communicate.

It is often misconceived that you can tell if a person is lying by analyzing their body language. Although you cannot directly tell if a person is lying, body language can help a person determine how another person feels.

There are certain rules about observing your target's body language. The most important is that you must determine their baseline or normal behavior. This helps prevent misinterpretation of what is normal behavior for your target or whether environmental factors such as temperature could be a factor. An example of this is when an individual crosses their arms across their body. This could show a target's discomfort or disagreement or it could simply be because they are cold.

Below are some interpretations for the most commonly seen body language.

| Target crosses their legs: | This position displays confidence or comfort. The target may also tilt towards the person they favor. |
|---|---|
| Torso blocking (crossed arms, etc): | This position displays discomfort/disagreement or the target just doesn't want to hear anymore. |
| Hands on hips: | This is a powerful territorial display or one that exerts authority or confidence. |
| Touching of neck area: | With this gesture, the target is trying to pacify themselves. They are uncomfortable, in doubt, or insecure about the current situation. |
| Eye blocking (with hands, eyelids, etc) | This position shows displeasure at what is happening or being said. |
| Increased eye blinking (beyond baseline behavior): | This occurs when your target is troubled, nervous or concerned. |

Table 4-1

The above table lists some of the more common body language gestures that can be seen. A great example of this is from Bill Clinton's testimony about the Monica Lewinski scandal. His eyes blink a lot faster than when you see him in a more comfortable setting such as the White House lawn. As we later learned, he was displaying the eye blinking gesture for being nervous because he was afraid of being exposed for lying. Be aware that just because someone is nervous does not mean they are lying.

Body language can reveal a lot about a target that even they may not know. If you plan to engage your target in a one on one conversation, be prepared to first get baseline behavior and then analyze their body language. You should then be able to start collecting information on what subject makes your target nervous or happy. When you have identified these things, you can then use elicitation to concentrate on the subject to help reveal more information.

One way to use body language without engaging your target is to do what is commonly referred to as "people watch." By watching your target you can start to pick up on schedules, mannerisms and preferences they may have. Perhaps your target prefers Burger King to McDonalds. By sitting, watching and analyzing your target's body language, you may learn whether the person they are meeting for lunch is a lover or just a business associate.

## On Their Person

Another avenue for information collection is looking at what your target has on their person. Including jewelry, the way they dress, the type of vehicle they drive and even what type of key chains they have. Observing what a target has on them is just as important as the target's body language.

One of the most basic examples of jewelry is the wedding ring. If a person is seen with a wedding ring, we can safely assume that this person is either married or engaged (maybe check their Facebook page to find a clue as to whom). Women tend to wear a wedding ring when engaged and married whereas men tend to wear a wedding band only when officially married. Although these are true in most cases, be cautious as your target may be recently divorced or widowed and may still be married emotionally. Also, just because someone doesn't wear a ring does not mean they are not married. There are certain anomalies that go along with this such a man may not like jewelry or a woman's wedding ring may be getting cleaned. As with all information collection, this information should not be taken with certainty until other information collected can be used to corroborate it.

Another great object that many people tend to forget or naively wear in public is an access badge for work.

Figure 4-1

Information Collected:

1. Full name
2. Place of employment

Some employers also display additional information on their badges such as level of security clearance. An access badge may not yield a wealth of information but it will help you get a lead. You could perhaps then browse the employer's website for your target's profile as shown in Chapter 1.

Another object that most people carry on them is a wallet or purse. If you can sidle up to your target while they have their wallet or purse open, perhaps in line at the grocery store, you can peek inside and collect information. Many people will carry a great deal of information in their wallet or purse such as pictures of their family, an out of state driver's license and banking information.

Figure 4-2

Information Collected

1. Club membership

Plastic cards can also yield information. Your target could be displaying membership to a wide variety of clubs and locations. A golf membership shows that the target enjoys playing golf whereas a library card shows the area where the target may live. In this situation, the individual in the figure above is holding a membership card to the FBI InfraGard. Further research shows that this is a joint FBI and civilian group meant to protect the United States' infrastructure.

Profiling a person can also help gather information on their background. Take a look at their clothing and personal vehicle. If your target is a Caucasian male age 45-55 with muddy work boots, a mossy oak camouflage jacket, Dickies jeans and pickup truck with camping gear in the back, you can probably say, with confidence, that your target is possibly a hunter and does not like rap music. Be cautious of any derogatory or negative stereotype because although stereotypes have a basis for being created, they were created to stereotype 100 percent of the group of people and there is always a large portion of that group that will not fit the stereotype.

# Defense

To defend against others eliciting information from you directly, you simply need to watch what you say and how much information you give away. There are many individuals that are trained to extract information from others without the target evening knowing.

With elicitation and social engineering you need to be aware of how these attacks are carried out and how to identify them. Once you identify that a person is either purposefully or unknowingly extracting information from you, you can either leave the situation or even fill the attackers head with misinformation. It is possible that the misinformation may put them off your trail but don't count on it.

NOTE: YOUR DEFENSIVE POSTURE AGAINST ELICITATION AND SOCIAL ENGINEERING SHOULD BE HEIGHTEND WHEN TRAVELING IN FOREIGN COUNTRIES.

Body language, although one can realize the positions they subconsciously choose, can be very hard to control all the time. Think of it as breathing or blinking your eyes. If you sit and think about the action, you can control it very easily, however it is very difficult, if not impossible, to control it all the time. This is another instance of simply being aware of your body position and how it may reveal something about how you are feeling at that moment.

Protecting against someone collecting information from your wallet, access badges and jewelry are things that you can consciously control and protect. There have been reports of identity thieves taking pictures of a person's credit card when at the checkout counter at a store. Because of this threat, you need to be aware of your surroundings.

# 5

# OTHER RESOURCES

There are many other resources that can be used to gather information about your target. It is only limited by your imagination and how much information your target is willing to give out or is even aware of.

Digging through a person's trash may not be desirable but it can yield a wealth of information. Just think of the things you throw away on a regular basis such an office/personal documents, birthday cards, food items and even medications.

Vehicles can also reveal information about a person. When someone decorates their car with a favorite sports team or political statements they are choosing to reveal information about themselves. This type of information can lead someone to form opinions about that person without even have met them. If someone has a strong dislike for that sports team or is of a different political viewpoint, that could hurt a potential relationship and could even lead to harassment or vandalism.

## Dumpster Diving

Dumpster diving, or going through someone's trash, is a very popular method of information collection and rightfully so. The amount of information yielded by dumpster diving is well worth the effort of getting dirty. In this section we will give a few examples of some things that may not be obvious.

## Plane Tickets

One item that people tend to discard without thinking is airplane tickets. Airplane tickets can help to reconstruct your target's journey, which most commonly, is round trip. By reconstructing your target's journey you can start to create (or confirm) an association matrix explained earlier. Your target may possibly have been in another city for business or pleasure. You can help determine which with other information you have collected about your target.

If your target travels often, they may travel for work. If they travel to their hometown (known from Facebook) they may be visiting parents, perhaps ill. If their location is a typical tourist destination, they may be on vacation. If their is more than one person on their itinerary, who is the other person? A friend, significant other, relative?

There are several websites such as www.flightaware.com and www.flightstats.com that can be used to trace your target's flights. Since you now have their tickets, you can plug in the relevant information, such as flight number and airline, and get more information about the flight itself. Also, don't forget that included on many (if not all) airline tickets is either a magnetic stripe or a bar code. Depending on the airline these can be read for possibly even more information about your target and their itinerary. Imagine getting the information an airline can about your target, especially in today's society of no-fly lists.

## Newspaper/Magazines

Newspapers and magazines can be an interesting find in a target's garbage. Immediately we may be able to gather information about our target. The following examples will help make you aware of information that can be gathered:

1. Foreign language – This may help determine if your target is foreign or may be attempting to learn another language.

2. Specific Interest Newspaper/Magazine – Magazine such as Tattoo Magazine or The Wall Street Journal. We can collect information about areas of interest or hobbies from these types of print.

3.  Circled items – Some individuals will circle items of interest when reading a newspaper or magazine. Doing this may help pinpoint information about your target. Circling an article about cancer may show that your target or a close friend or family may have cancer. Circling a job listing may show that your target (or family member) may be seeking employment. The type of job itself may also yield information about your target inferring about their level and type of education.

## Grocery/Health Habits

Information about your target can be gathered by the food they consume. Carefully look at your target's discarded food and food containers. Is the food mostly healthy or unhealthy? How many alcoholic containers are there and what type? Does your target smoke? How often and what brand? What flavor of ice cream to they enjoy? This can help give you a basic understanding of their day-to-day habits. Keep in mind that trash is usually collected once a week in most areas.

Another thing to collect from the trash to learn more about your target's health are prescription drug containers. In 1996 the Health Insurance Portability and Accountability Action or HIPAA was enacted by Congress to help address privacy and security issues relating to healthcare records. However, if your target discards their empty prescription bottles into the trash (which eventually becomes public) HIPAA cannot protect them. If anti-depressant medications are found with your target's name on the bottle, you have now collected part of their medical history.

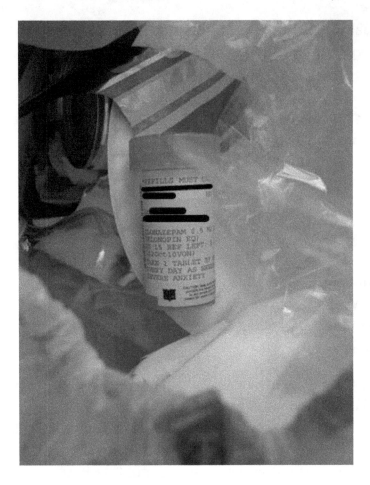

Figure 5-1

Information Collected:

1. Medical health of target
2. Target's doctor and possible medical facility


Although illegal, a person may be blackmailed, denied medical care or fired from a job because of medical conditions. Do you really want a person on heavy medication for anxiety (pictured above) or severe depression working with firearms or weapons? Do you want a person with Hepatitis, a blood transmitted disease, working as a chef at a restaurant?

Take the example of if you were in a car accident. If the person whom you hit was suing you, they may hire a private detective to find out more information about you. If the investigator finds a prescription bottle in your trash, which requires you to dose three times daily and not operate a vehicle, you may very well lose the case.

# Vehicles

People may not realize but their vehicles can reveal quite a bit of information about them. Besides the make and model car your target owns (young, single men without children usually do not drive minivans), stickers reveal information about your target.

## Work Decals

One example of a work sticker is a Department of Defense registration sticker. This sticker reveals much more information than an affiliation with the DoD. These stickers are color coordinated and also show what base the vehicle was last registered at. Here is an example of a DoD sticker.

Figure 5-2

As this book is printed in black and white, you are unable to see the color codes. In the above example however, the color-coding will appear on the background of the base of registration, in this case HICKAM AFB or Hickam Air Force Base in Honolulu, Hawaii. Because of the location of the base, we know our target has spent some time in Hawaii. We can narrow the time our target spent in Hawaii by the registration expiration date, in this example it is September of 2011. Below are the different color codes of the DoD stickers.

| Officer | Blue background with white letters. |
|---|---|
| Enlisted | Red background with white letters. |
| Civilian | Green background with white letters. |
| Contractor | White background with black letters. |

Table 5-1

In addition to having a DoD sticker on your target's vehicle, higher ranking members of the military also display their rank. This is used for benefits such as better parking on military installations.

Figure 5-3

Information Collected:

1. Approximate time in the military (Usually around 20 years for higher ranks)
2. Approximate base salary (Military pay records are public)
3. If enlisted, target's branch of service determined by insignia

## Bumper Stickers and Decals

There are many types of bumper stickers and decals out there including simple pictures and whimsical sayings. However, different types of bumper stickers can also reveal information about your target. Since anyone can print a bumper sticker, the possibilities are endless. Some of the most common are stickers for university attended and political association or beliefs. Some of the more revealing ones such as parking permits for residential communities and advertising where your children attend school.

**ALERT: Be cautious of city parking permits with vicinity codes and "Honor Student" bumper stickers (Figure 5-9). Parking permits can help narrow down the area where you live. At this point, the only thing a malicious individual has to do is stroll your neighborhood looking for your vehicle. Even worse with "Honor Student" stickers is advertising where your child attends school. Although living in a certain area sometimes determines where your children attend school, you do not want to give away any information that may put your children in harms way. Do everything you can from displaying these stickers. You can find more help in the Defense section at the end of this chapter.

Here are some examples:

Figure 5-4

Information Collected:

1. University target (or family member) attended

Figure 5-5

Information Collected:

1. Political party affiliation (the probability rating goes up when more stickers of the same political party are present)

Figure 5-6

1. Target's Religion and values (above the radio frequency it says "Catholic Radio in the Northwest")

Figure 5-7

Information Collected:

1. University attendance and years
2. City of past/current residence

    The above image only S.J.U. but a quick Google search will show Saint Joseph's University and Saint John's University. By looking at the web site of each university, we can say with a fair degree of accuracy that it is Saint Josephs because of their overuse of the acronym SJU. In this case, we are given a bonus in that we can probably speculate to our target's religion because of the Mission Statement of the school.

Figure 5-8

Information Collected:

1. Location of target's residence
2. POSSIBLE end to target's apartment lease as determined by expiration date (this would only apply to rental communities)

Figure 5-9

Information Collected:

1. School attended by target's child/children
2. Location of residence by school district

Increasing in popularity is the decals of the stick figure family. Sometimes these stickers can give away a lot of information such as full names of family members.

Figure 5-10

Information Collected:

1. Family name
2. Every family members first name

The combination of information from the sticker in Figure 5-9 and Figure 5-10 sticker could have devastating consequences including a targeted kidnapping.

## License Plates

Often times when an individual purchases a car at a dealership, a license plate frame advertising that dealership will be attached to the license plate. Many times people will replace these with another one they have purchased. If your target places a license plate frame on their vehicle with a sports team, you can determine that your target is a fan of that sports team. The following image is an example of a dealerships license plate frame.

Figure 5-11

Information Collected:

1. General area of purchase of vehicle

The information of where the vehicle was purchased can be important because, in this example, California is a big state. This information narrows down the possible residence of the target or some type of connection to the area, such as Lake Tahoe.

License plate numbers themselves can reveal information about a target. Many websites are available to lookup license plate numbers and the information associated with them such as name and address of the owner.

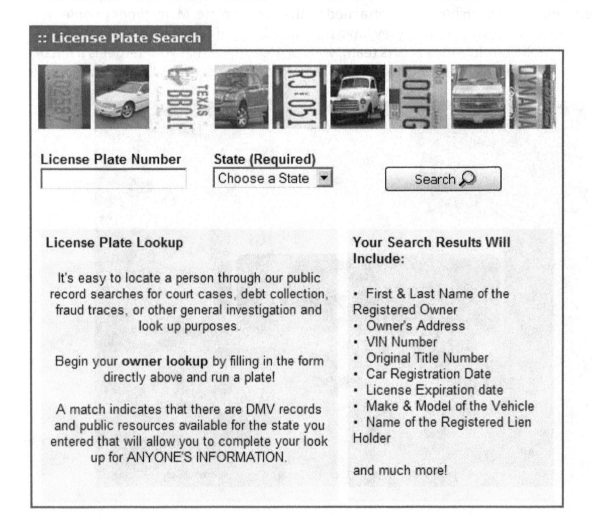

Figure 5-12

Information Collected:

1. Full name of vehicle owner
2. Address of owner
3. Car registration information

NOTE: Looking up a license plate number is illegal in most states without at least law enforcement certifications. This book is only to illustrate that the possibility exists to gather information in this manner.

An obvious way, but one people don't often think about, in which a target will give away information is trash and/or paperwork left in the open inside of their vehicle. Many people will leave information unprotected in their vehicle without thinking about the type of information that is left on it. Perhaps your target just came out of the doctor's office with some paperwork and puts it on the passenger seat when getting into the car. You can collect information from this paperwork when your target goes into the grocery store quickly on the way home.

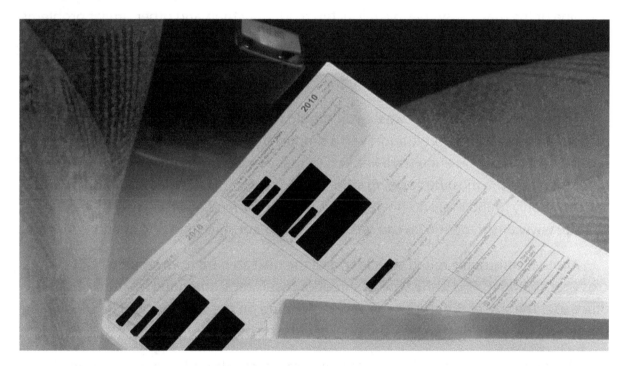

Figure 5-13

Information Collected:

1. Target's Social Security Number
2. Previous or current employment
3. Tax withholdings

# Defense

## Shredders

Defending against dumpster diving is very similar to defending against identity theft. You should shred every piece of paper that you discard. Almost every piece of paper with something written or printed on it has the potential to reconstruct a portion of your life, no matter how small. A phone number or address with no name can be traced, a password can be kept for later and tried on websites that you visit, and package labels show your relationship with a person or business.

One of the major ways people fall victim to identify theft and other similar problems is simply by failing to destroy important documents. All an identity thief would have to do is dig through your trash (whether in front of your house or at the dump), and find a document with the necessary information.

To properly destroy paper waste you should use a shredder. I personally recommend shredding everything. Even a simple letter from a company saying they received your inquiry is enough to link you to that company. Shredders come in three different types, the most basic being strip-cut shredders. These types of shredders are still commonly found in stores however I would recommend against using them. The website www.unshredder.com can reconstruct strip-cut shredded documents with ease.

Another commonly found shredder, and the next step up from strip-cut, is the cross-cut shredder. This is the type of shredder that is recommended for home and office use. The size of the stripes can vary depending on the shredder and depending on the sensitivity of the documents, the smaller cuts the better.

The next step up in shredders is known as micro-cut shredders or obliterators. These are typically used to destroy classified material and can turn an 8.5x11 inch sheet of paper into 6,000 to about 12,000 pieces. Another way, the best way, government organizations destroy paper waste is burn them, which is the only true way to destroy paper waste.

If shredders aren't available at the time you need to discard something and cant wait until you get home, rip up the papers into the smallest pieces possible and separate them in different trashcans, preferably at different establishments.

## Vehicle Stickers

Bumper stickers are mainly based upon pride. A mother is proud of the university her daughter is attending, a person of their political views, or even of the radio station they listen to. The simple defense against this type of information collection is to simply not place these stickers on your vehicle. It's simply not necessary. Of course this is up to you on how much you are willing to share with the world but be cautious of the things you share. If you are not willing to go up to a stranger and tell them which way you lean politically then don't post it on your vehicle.

Some stickers however may be unavoidable such as parking permits and access stickers. Unfortunately many places that issue these types of stickers have requirements for where they are placed and restrictions on how to place them. However, if your permit issuer has no such limitations, you can place the sticker on a 3x5 card or another removal item. An example of one is below.

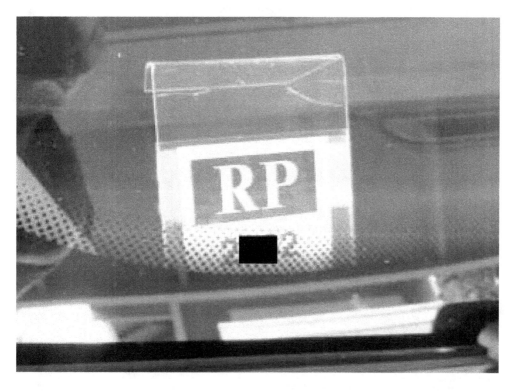

Figure 5-14

The above picture shows two great defensive measures when it comes to parking permits. First, the vehicle owner has placed the parking permit on a piece of plastic not attached to the vehicle. This way whenever they vehicle is not parked in the owners apartment complex, it can be removed and placed elsewhere.

Second, the apartment complex has done it tenants a real favor. Instead of putting the full name of the complex on its parking permit (like Figure 5-8), it has only put the complex's initials. It is now much more difficult for someone to identify where a vehicle's owner lives.

# 6

# SOCIAL ENGINEERING

Social engineering can be defined as the act of manipulating an individual to do what you ask of them. This commonly comes in the form of collecting information or gaining physical access to an area otherwise off limits. Social Engineering takes advantage of human nature. The social engineer will target a person's desire to be helpful, be greedy, avoid confrontation and avoid embarrassment. Social engineering has been written about, discussed and blogged ad nauseam and this book will only cover a small portion of it.

Now that you are done collecting information on your target, social engineering could be the next phase of your offensive. The information you collected from the previous chapters can help gain the trust of the target of the social engineering attack. If you wanted to gain access to an individual's office, knowing about where his children go to school, his wife's name, and how often he smokes can help you show his secretary that you know him personally and that it is probably okay to let you into his office unescorted.

## Types of Social Engineering

There are six types of social engineering that you can use to obtain your goal. In this chapter, the word "target" will refer to the individual you are directly using the social engineering attack against. For example, if you collected information about a company CEO, your social engineering target could be their assistant.

**Authority** – One of the more popular social engineering attacks is when the attacker asserts themselves as having more authority than the target. By doing this you do three things, intimidate the target, make the target think you actually do have more authority and/or put so much pressure on the target they make a quick and rash decision. In the last case, the easiest way for the target to relieve the stress would be to just allow you into the restricted area.

**Liking** – This technique works on the premise that as humans, we are willing to do more for individuals we like and feel a connection with. As the attacker you could put your target in the position of the helper or you can try to find commonalities and exploit them.

**Reciprocation** – Reciprocation is exactly what it means by giving something for getting something. This method also exploits a human trait. People naturally feel compelled to give something in return if they receive something such as a gift, advice, or favor from you.

**Social Validation** – This method works on the premise that most individuals in a group/company/society are doing something, so why do something out of the norm. The target wants to do what everyone around them is doing. This is the basis for the saying "everyone else is doing it."

**Consistency** - People prefer to be consistent because it is more convenient and usually requires less work.

**Scarcity** – This method expresses to the target of your social engineering attack that an item is in short supply or emergency need. If the item is in emergency need, and it affects the target, they may provide it so they are not inconvenienced. A popular example of scarcity is used in marketing with "Buy now, quantities are limited."

With these six methods of social engineering comes different ways in which to deliver them. Below are the four most common methods of delivery. The way to employ social engineering is only limited by the attacker's imagination.

1. Person-to-Person – This delivery method is when the attacker will approach the target face to face. The most common is the pizza guy slipping past the security guard as seen in many movies.

2. Computer Based – This delivery method uses the Internet as a medium. Most common occurrences of this are pop-up windows, spam email with attachments, and phishing attacks.

3. Reverse social engineering – This method is a bit trickier as it involves sabotaging a piece of equipment and then offering to fix it, effectively gaining access.

4. Telephone – Using the telephone is a great to engage a target. It gives the target confidence that it could be an authentic call as well as giving the attacker confidence by not being face to face. To make a phone call more authentic, an attacker can use caller identification spoofing.

An example of a person-to-person attack can be seen in many movies such as Beverly Hills Cop. In this movie, Eddie Murphy attempts to gain access to a high scale restaurant. To bypass the maître d', Murphy acts like a homosexual and tells him that he would like to speak with Victor Maitland and unless he allows him to pass, the maître d' himself will have to inform Victor that he may have contracted a venereal disease. This works due to putting the maître d' in an awkward situation to where he will just let Murphy pass through instead of having to deliver the news himself.

Using a telephone is a very effective and popular method to deliver social engineering attacks. To help the authenticity of a phone call, an attacker can use caller identification spoofing. A great example of this is if an attacker called up an office worker and asked for their password. The attacker could spoof the number of the helpdesk to seem more authentic. Although the practice of caller ID spoofing has now been deemed illegal in the Unites States by Truth in Caller ID Act of 2010, it can still be done.

"Sometimes, I just don't want them to know it's me calling.."

"..I call someone from my phone, and the person's caller ID displays a number that I intend them to see. My privacy is protected. Simple as that!" More Stories >>

Ready To Spoof Your Caller ID?

**Buy SpoofCard Credits!**

NEW SMS Spoofing!

Figure 6-1. www.spoofcard.com

Now that we've covered social engineering, you may be able to come up with scenarios that combine the information you have collected on someone, social engineering and a well defined goal or motivation. Using the information you have collected, you will be able to sound and look more confident when employing social engineering attacks. If the target does something that is unexpected, you will now be able to respond appropriately because of the research you have previously done on your target.

# Defense

The only way to defend against social engineering is to simply be aware of the techniques and methods. If you can identify that a social engineering is taking place, you can ask a person to verify their identity. If you are in an office building, employees should be required to wear some type of identification.

If you identify an attack against you over the phone, simply ask the person the name of their company and if you can call them back. You can then verify the number displayed on the caller identification with the company's phone number on the website. You should then call the phone number on the company's official website and ask the authenticity of the call.

The phone verification can work in the same method as a phishing attack over email. If you receive an email seemingly from your bank asking you to verify information, NEVER click on any links in the email. If you are unsure whether or not the email is authentic, type in your bank's address into a web browser or call them to verify.

Social engineering continues to be the number one security vulnerability for companies. This is because humans are often thought of as the weakest link and will always make mistakes. If you can identify a social engineering attack, you can deter it.

# ABOUT THE AUTHOR

Andrew Meyers has extensive education and experience in information security. This includes a Masters degree from Norwich University, designated a Center of Academic Excellence by the National Security Agency. Andy has also served in the military under special operations with an intelligence gathering mission. Among his many hobbies such as hiking and surfing, traveling the world and learning new cultures is at the top.

www.ingramcontent.com/pod-product-compliance
Lightning Source LLC
Chambersburg PA
CBHW060448060326
40689CB00020B/4468